OPPRESSION:
A Socio-History
of Black-White
Relations
in America

OPPRESSION:
A Socio-History of Black-White Relations in America

**Jonathan H. Turner
Royce Singleton, Jr.
David Musick**

Nelson-Hall nh Chicago

LIBRARY OF CONGRESS CATALOGING IN PUBLICATION DATA

Turner, Jonathan H.
  Oppression : a socio-history of Black-White relations
in America.

  Bibliography: p.
  Includes index.
  1. United States—Race relations. 2. Racism—United States. 3. Afro-Americans—Civil rights. I. Singleton, Royce. II. Musick, David. III. Title.
E185.615.T847 1984   305.8'00973   83-25061
ISBN 0–8304–1074–0 (cloth)

ISBN 0–8304–1117–8 (paper)

Copyright © 1984 by Jonathan H. Turner

Manufactured in the United States of America

10 9 8 7 6 5 4 3 2 1

The paper in this book is pH neutral (acid-free).

Contents

CHAPTER ONE:

The Nature
of Oppression

This book is about oppression of black Americans by white Americans. Perhaps the term "oppression" is too strong and value-laden for some, but it captures the essence of our topic. Indeed, we have deliberately chosen this term because other concepts on "race and ethnic relations" do not effectively communicate our subject matter. Terms like "prejudice," "discrimination," "ethnic antagonism," and "racism" all denote properties of "oppression," but they do not adequately embrace the topic of this book. In this short opening chapter, therefore, we will attempt to clarify the concept of oppression and indicate how it allows us to organize data and theoretical constructs.

A General Definition of Oppression

We will begin with a general definition of oppression and then outline its relationship to other concepts that occupy analysts' attention when studying race and ethnic relations. At the most general level, oppression can be defined as a situation in which one, or more, identifiable segments of the population in a social system systematically and successfully

act over a prolonged period of time to prevent another identifiable segment, or segments, of the population from attaining
access to the scarce and valued resources of that system.

There are several key terms in this definition that we should
underscore. First, oppression is a situation that endures over
a "prolonged period of time." Second, it involves "systematic"
efforts of an "identifiable population" to limit the actions of
others. That is, oppression is a self-conscious process by specific people in particular contexts; it is not the unanticipated
result of unconscious social processes. Third, such efforts must
be "successful" if a situation of oppression is to exist. Fourth,
because oppression denies access of one or more segments of
a population to "scarce and valued" resources, it is a dimension of more general stratification processes in a society.

Oppression and Stratification

Oppression must be viewed as a specific type of stratifying
process in social systems. Our initial task, therefore, is to examine briefly the relationship between oppression and stratification. In all social systems, some resources are defined as
more valuable than others. Three of the most valuable resources in human societies are material well-being, power, and
prestige. Stratification is both a structural and a processual
concept in that it denotes all those processes (1) that are involved in the unequal distribution of material well-being,
power, and prestige; and (2) that create a comparatively enduring system of ranks that divide the population of a society
in terms of their relative degrees of access to scarce and valued
resources (Turner, 1978:328-32; Turner and Starnes, 1976;
Turner, 1984).

As a dimension of stratification, oppression is both a process
and a structure. At the procedural level, it involves specific
acts by some people that are designed to place others in the
lower ranks of a society. At the structural level, such processes
create a bottom rank in a hierarchical system of ranks. The
members of this bottom rank are the victims of oppression and
are likely to organize their lives around the fact that they will
possess few valuable resources. "Caste" is a term that is often

used to describe a system of stratification that reveals little mobility in and out of all ranks.[1] In a caste system, not all castes are "victims" of oppression in that some castes enjoy high degrees of access to resources. Indeed, these higher castes sometimes enjoy the spoils of oppression by extracting the products of the oppressed populations' labor. At other times, they receive benefits by virtue of their not having to compete with the oppressed since the latter are excluded from key, resource-laden positions. Thus, only the lowest ranks in a caste system are the victims of oppression.

In American society, oppression often occurs in comparatively open stratification systems where social mobility across at least some ranks is possible and frequent.[2] In such systems, a "caste-like" situation prevails for a segment of the population, as has been the case in America for blacks. Oppression and caste are separate dimensions of stratification systems, although lower castes are often the result of oppressive processes. As we will stress in later chapters, black-white relations in America have historically involved relegation and confinement of blacks to the lowest rank in the stratification system, thereby denying them access to material well-being, power, and prestige. As long as we recognize the limitations involved, we can term the plight of blacks "caste-like."

We should emphasize that oppression does not always lead to relegation to the lowest ranks. Some victims of oppression can be denied both power and prestige, but can occupy middle ranks in terms of their access to material well-being. For example, Asians in America such as the Japanese were initially denied access to power and prestige but were allowed to accumulate wealth as long as their activities were confined to a limited range of roles. Similarly, Jews in Europe and elsewhere have, until recently, been denied power but allowed to gather some educational prestige and wealth from economic activities. The existence of such "middleman minorities" in many societies attests to the fact that oppressive acts can be selective with respect to only some scarce resources (Bonacich, 1977; Bonacich and Turner, 1980). Thus, like all social processes, oppression varies by degree: the more complete the denial of all three universal resources—material well-being, power, and prestige—the greater is the oppression. Conversely, the less successful are efforts at denial of any or all three resources, then the less is the oppression.

Oppressive Acts and Attitudes

The specific acts by members of one population that oppress others will vary widely depending upon the particular context. The potential plethora of acts are usually viewed as elements of a process termed "discrimination." Discrimination occurs when criteria that are irrelevant to performance in a situation are used to encourage the successful accomplishment of goals for one set of individuals who meet these criteria and to discourage such accomplishments for those who do not meet these criteria. For most jobs, such factors as merit, ability, and experience are the relevant standards for evaluating job candidates. If an irrelevant criterion such as "color of skin" and its degree of "whiteness" are used, so that whites are hired and blacks are not, then discrimination has occurred. Discrimination does not always lead to oppression. When discriminatory acts are consistent, long-term, systematic, and successful in denying access of one segment of a population to scarce and valuable resources, then discrimination results in oppression.

What makes discriminatory acts consistent, long-term, systematic, and successful? Several variables are involved, including: (1) the degree to which an oppressed population can be readily identified, (2) the degree of emotional arousal of oppressors, (3) the respective degrees of power of the oppressed and oppressors, and (4) the degree to which oppression can be institutionalized in key social structures and prevailing cultural beliefs.

Identification

It is difficult to discriminate against a population that cannot be readily identified. Distinctive social, cultural, and biological attributes can all serve as a basis for labeling targets of oppression. But when a population can be identified biologically in terms of skin color or facial features, then discrimination becomes easier. Even if objective biological distinctions cannot be made, oppressors often construct myths about biological differences, viewing the targets of discrimination as a distinctive "race." For example, Jews could not by any stretch of the biological imagination be considered a race, although their presumed biological distinctiveness has been used as a basis for intense discrimination. The fact that Hitler needed to mark Jews with a visible emblem documents the social construction of presumed biological differences.

Other sources of distinction—such as language and accents, behavior patterns, values, and beliefs—can all serve as a basis of oppression, but since these can be changed, they serve less effectively. If discrimination can be used to maintain the distinctive social and cultural patterns of a population, then a vicious cycle can extend the pattern of oppression. Initial distinctions are used as a basis for labeling and for discrimination; the targets of discrimination then retreat into the comfort of their cultural and social patterns; and the maintenance of these patterns serves to make them visible targets for their oppressors.

All other things being equal, the more readily identifiable a population, the more it can potentially be the subject of discriminatory acts. And the more the characteristics that make a population the target of discrimination cannot be eliminated, the more likely are discriminatory acts to endure and become oppressive.

Emotional Arousal

Why would people seek to discriminate against others? And why would they maintain patterns of discrimination? At the psychological level, people must be motivated and emotionally aroused to discriminate. This raises the additional question: What forces generate such arousal? The answer appears to revolve around the degree to which a target population is perceived to threaten the well-being of potential discriminators. The greater the level of threat experienced, the more likely are people to be aroused emotionally and attuned to the distinctive features of a target population.

Perceptions of threat can be generated under diverse social conditions. In general, if two identifiable populations compete for limited resources, such as jobs and living space, then each will be more likely to see the other as a threat, and the one with the greater power will discriminate. Sometimes, of course, threat is generated artificially through the actions of political leaders who label an identifiable population as a "threat" and, in so doing mobilize people to a particular cause. Such was the case, for example, with Hitler and the Jews as well as with white Americans and the Chinese in the post-railroad-building era (Bonacich, 1973).

Power Differences

Differences in power among identifiable populations are also essential to effective discrimination. If a target population possesses power, it can resist discrimination. The more equal in power two populations, the less likely is discrimination. What determines respective degrees of power? Many variables influence power, such as the size of a population, the extent to which it provides valued resources, the degree of its organization, and the resources that it can use to press for its interests. These last two criteria are particularly important. Historically, large populations—like slaves that provided valued labor services—have been oppressed, because their oppressors created social arrangements that prevented the accumulation of resources and that stymied organization. For example, the plantation system in America represented one such set of arrangements that kept slaves powerless.

Institutionalizing Discrimination

For discriminatory acts to result in a pattern of oppression, they must become "institutionalized." By institutionalized, we have two things in mind. First, social structures, particularly economic and political institutions, must be constructed in ways that actively encourage discrimination. Second, a system of beliefs that legitimates these structures must be developed. For unless structured patterns of discrimination seem "right and proper" in the eyes of those who discriminate, these structures will not endure. Indeed, they can be effectively resisted and challenged. Unless people hold attitudes that condone and encourage discrimination against a population, oppression will not endure.

Such attitudes are often termed "prejudices" because their main characteristic is to highlight what are considered negative and undesirable traits in the target population. Prejudices are both a cause and a consequence of discriminatory actions. When people hold prejudices, they are more likely to discriminate if the opportunity presents itself. Conversely, prejudice can be the result of discrimination, as people seek to rationalize their acts. Whichever way the causal arrow goes, the critical point is that discrimination and prejudice go together.[3]

Summary

Discriminatory acts are likely to result in oppression under the following conditions (Bonacich, 1972; Van der Zanden, 1972):

1. when a social system reveals populations that are biologically, culturally, and/or socially distinguishable;
2. when one population perceives another as a threat to its well-being, particularly when
   a. there is competition over scarce resources, and
   b. political leaders need to unify a population by focusing on a common enemy;
3. when populations possess vastly unequal degrees of power; and
4. when discriminatory actions can become institutionalized in specific social structures and in cultural beliefs that legitimate these structures.

Stated in this way, these conditions do not offer many details. They simply present us with a general view of when we can expect oppression to occur. The purpose of this book is to fill in many of the details by analyzing one historical case of oppression and using this case as a basis for more extensive theorizing.

Racial Oppression in America

While biologists legitimately feel uncomfortable in distinguishing among "the races," ordinary people do not. Indeed, one of the most salient dimensions in human interaction is a person's "race." It is not surprising, therefore, that entire populations are distinguished by their "race" and that such distinctions become an initial basis for discrimination. In a "white society," it would be hard not to notice "blacks" as distinctive, especially when imported as slaves and subjected to the indignities of plantation systems. All other things being equal, a population that can be distinguished biologically and that evidences distinctive social and cultural patterns is a likely target for discrimination, especially if the other conditions of oppression are met.

When this biologically distinguishable population poses a threat—whether actual or contrived—then discrimination will increase, particularly when this population has little power. For instance, the large concentrations of slave labor posed an economic threat to southern white labor, who saw blacks as willing to work for less if they ever gained their freedom. Labor thus became "shock troops" for maintaining the patterns of oppression that existed in the South during the pre- and post-Civil War periods. Thus, slavery and the plantation system had the curious consequence of providing wealth to large farmers and affluence to smaller farmers who could afford slaves, while at the same time threatening the white labor force whose already low wages could be undercut should slaves, or ex-slaves, enter the job market. And in the North, this threat became real as industrialists used ex-slaves as strikebreakers.

The existence of slavery and the plantation system represented a well-institutionalized set of social structural arrangements that became legitimated by cultural beliefs. Later, acts of discrimination against blacks in the post-Civil War era also became structured and culturally legitimated. Once "race" becomes the criterion for institutionalization of discrimination, we can visualize this situation as racial oppression. In America, blacks could be readily identified; they posed both real and imagined threats to large segments of the population; and they had no power when imported as slaves. Hence, discrimination became institutionalized in a series of concrete structural arrangements and cultural beliefs.

This book is devoted to tracing the history of such racial

oppression of blacks. Our goal is to trace the history of institutionalized discrimination against blacks that resulted in, and
to a large extent still perpetuates, their relegation to the bottom
ranks in the stratification system. To do this, we will first
present a review of the beliefs that have been used to legitimate
discriminatory structural arrangements. Then, we will review
the history of those arrangements in economic, political, legal,
and educational structures that have limited the options of
blacks. Finally, we will attempt to expand upon the very general statements in this chapter by developing some tentative
theoretical propositions on the process of oppression.[4]

CHAPTER TWO:

The Culture of Black Oppression[1]

In June 1942, the following question was first asked in a national survey: "In general, do you think Negroes are as intelligent as white people; that is, can they learn just as well if they are given the same education (and training)?" Responses to this question reveal the scope of America's culture of racism at that time: 42 percent of the respondents across the country said yes; 48 percent said no; and 10 percent said they did not know (Simon, 1974:57). Over two hundred years earlier, American colonists debated a similar question concerning the capacity of black slaves to learn the principles of religion necessary for their conversion to Christianity. Although we will never know exactly what the colonists thought and said about this issue, the available evidence shows that most believed blacks to be ignorant and unteachable (Jordan, 1968:187-90).

This correspondence between eighteenth- and twentieth-century beliefs is not a case of history repeating itself. The correspondence assumes heightened significance when we consider that the capacity for religious experience was extremely important in the eighteenth century, as "intelligence" is today. Indeed, the assumption of black "inferiority" has been a basic tenet of American culture for three hundred and fifty

11

years. Understanding its origin and tenacity means understanding the history of racial beliefs in America. As noted in the last chapter, oppression can endure only if it is legitimated by cultural beliefs. To understand the history of black oppression, it is necessary to review those systems of cultural beliefs that have sustained patterns of discrimination.

Precolonial English Beliefs

The origins of American racial beliefs can be traced to Elizabethan England, where English culture formed the preconceptions that shaped the early colonists' initial reactions to blacks. Winthrop Jordan (1968) identifies several aspects of these preconceptions, beginning with English impressions of the African's "blackness." Early descriptions of Africans related by travelers almost always began with accounts of their complexion, and the fact that the exaggerated term "black" was used suggests a powerful impact upon English perceptions. At this time, the concept "blackness" connoted baseness, evil, danger, and repulsion, whereas whiteness connoted such things as virtue, beneficence, peace, and beauty. Thus, Africans were most readily identified in terms of a color that accentuated their distinctiveness in negative overtones.

Religious speculations frequently offered "explanations" of African blackness in a way that confirmed African inferiority. For example, the adventurer George Best gave biblical authority to negative conceptions about Africans by reference to a story in Genesis, chapters 9 and 10, in which Noah places a curse upon Canaan, the son of Ham, making him a "servant of servants." Although the tale logically implies slavery but says nothing about skin color, Best concluded that a curse of blackness upon Ham's son and all his descendants accounted for the color of Africans. Such a belief was buttressed by African "heathenism." Christianity, which still occupied a central place in European society, held other religions to be defective and inferior. To the English, who identified Protestant Christianity with English nationalism, heathenism was not easily separable from the African's other attributes. As Jordan (1968:23) notes: "Being a Christian was not merely a matter of subscribing to certain doctrines; it was a quality inherent in oneself and in one's society. It was interconnected with all the other attributes of normal and proper men."

English ethnocentrism expressed itself in many other ways as well. Travelers took an active interest in the details of purported savagery, and by English standards of clothing, housing, language, government, and morality, African culture was inevitably found to be uncivilized. An important facet of these impressions was the tendency to describe African behavior as "bestial." As Jordan points out, the terms "bestial" and "beastly" had strong sexual connotations in Elizabethan England, and such terms were used widely in English accounts of West Africa. In addition, English people's introduction "to the anthropoid apes and to Negroes at the same time and in the same place" and the longstanding myths associating apes with the devil, with evil, with sexual sin—and with blackness—caused much speculation about the relationship between apes and Negroes. One common notion, for example, was that sexual union sometimes occurred between apes and Negroes.

In short, to the English, virtually every characteristic of the African invited invidious distinctions. Whether in terms of color, religion, or style of life, Africans were seen as strikingly different and inferior, so radically different as to be considered subhuman savages who engaged in bestial forms of behavior. This extremely negative image was given legitimacy through the ethnocentric prism of English society[2]; and the impact of such an image was to be profound. For as long as Africans were considered as less than human, the moral precepts of Protestant religion were not violated and inhuman practices would be defined as humane. Such was the case as the English settled in America and the first Americans began to oppress blacks.

Racial Beliefs in Colonial America

The first twenty Africans to arrive in America were traded for food supplies by a Dutch man-of-war that put into Jamestown in 1619. Although they were bound over for some form of servitude, the precise status of Africans in America is not known until the 1660s, when "Negroes" were declared slaves by Virginia and Maryland statutes. Consequently, whether racial prejudice made slavery possible, or whether slavery was produced largely by economic forces and then fostered racism, has been hotly debated by historians (see, for example, Degler, 1959; Fredrickson, 1971b; Handlin and Handlin, 1950; Jordan, 1962). The most sensible position is that, like racist beliefs and institutions in contemporary society, slavery and prejudice were mutually reinforcing. It is difficult to see how racial slavery could have evolved if English colonists had not made invidious distinctions between themselves and Africans before their initial contact. It is also clear that this image was reinforced by the development of slavery in America and was elaborated into an extensive belief system.

The Rise of Racial Slavery

English conceptions of various forms of servitude appear to have been crucial to the evolution of America's unique brand of racial slavery. The colonists were familiar in 1619 with other types of bondage. Many early settlers paid for their ocean passage by means of indentured servitude. Indentures were negotiable, transferable contracts that bound one person to serve another for a period of usually four to seven years. They did not involve a complete loss of personal freedom, however, since there were reciprocal obligations between master and servant, with servants possessing certain social and legal rights. This type of bondage was clearly differentiated from slavery, which was at the time a perpetual condition of servitude for certain prisoners and captives of war. Implying as it did a particularly degrading status, "slave" was also an epithet for the basest kind of person.

Long before 1619, the English also had some knowledge, albeit imprecise, of the slave trade conducted by the Spanish and the Portuguese. They knew that large numbers of blacks, allegedly captured in African tribal wars, were being transported to New World settlements for enslavement. More importantly, they tended to associate the slavery practiced in these settlements exclusively with the hereditary, lifetime service forced upon Africans.[3] Whether or not they themselves adopted this practice from the time of their first contact with Africans, the English clearly had in mind the kind of distinctions that could foster the institution of slavery based upon race. Adding to this the need for labor, as well as the vulnerability of Africans dislodged from their homeland without the protection of indentures, it is easy to understand how black slavery evolved in colonial America.

Soon after the statutory recognition of slavery, various laws, or slave codes, were passed stripping blacks of their rights until, by the early 1700s, they were no longer defined as legal persons but as chattel property—little more than "beasts of burden." This rapid institutionalization of slavery was to have profound effects on the history of racial attitudes in America, for the subordinate position in which blacks were placed served to reinforce colonists' preconceptions of the African's "inferiority" and to preclude blacks' ability to win the respect of whites. Once this cycle of interaction between slavery and supporting beliefs was set in motion, it was to require constant revision and elaboration as slaveholders faced a host of problems and challenges.

The Attitude of the Church

The church continued to have a significant though paradoxical effect on racial attitudes during this period. African heathenism was an important point of distinction in colonists' first impressions. However, the church, with its universalistic, proselytizing nature and its assumption of spiritual equality among humans, could have had a salutary influence. Among the reasons it did not was the fact that many of the clergy who advocated Christianizing Africans also endorsed slavery. More important, conversions were infrequent. In New England, where the church was strong, there were few blacks, and the exclusionist strain in Puritanism tended to circumvent the process of conversion. In the South, where the church was less central to everyday affairs, the failure to convert was probably due in part to the practical problems of instruction required for conversion to the Protestant church. Some southerners also believed that conversion would make blacks worse slaves, while others contended that blacks did not have the capacity for religious experience.

Resistance to the religious conversion of slaves continued to set them apart from English people in a vital way until about 1740. At this time a wave of religious revivals created a radical shift in church policy, and blacks entered the church in increasing numbers. The admission of spiritual equality with blacks eventually joined hands with secular beliefs about liberty and equality to create a dilemma that was a source of heated controversy from the revolutionary era to the Civil War. However, physical distinctions had assumed central importance by the time religious equality arrived, enabling whites to justify continued enslavement of their "Christian brothers."

A Shift in Terminology

The emphasis on physiognomy is partially revealed by the shift in terminology in the 1600s. The distinction between "Negro" and "Christian" became a distinction between "Negro" and "English." Then, the latter term became interchangeable with "free" and "white." Finally, after 1700, the term "white" was adopted to unmistakably designate the racial distinction. For the most part, however, these distinctions preceded nineteenth- and twentieth-century "scientific" racism.

With the development of the Linnaean system of classification, people began to impose a hierarchy on the orders of species. Several scholars also theorized about gradations among varieties of human beings based upon physical distinctions. In this process, skin color and culture were invariably linked; and with Europeans doing the ranking, the cultural superiority of whites over blacks was a foregone conclusion.

Sexual Fears

The colonial period also saw the rise of a complex set of attitudes about interracial sex. Although miscegenation was a common practice in the early 1700s—especially in the South, where white men far outnumbered white women—it was nonetheless perceived as a threat to individual morality and cultural integrity. Miscegenation was outlawed in Virginia and

Maryland at about the same time that they legally instituted slavery. By the time of the American Revolution, all the colonies had prohibited interracial sexual relations and intermarriage.

The continued sexual exploitation of black women by white men seems to have engendered a strong sense of guilt, expressed in beliefs about lascivious black women and well endowed, sexually aggressive black men. As Jordan (1968) suggests, white assumptions about the black woman's sexual responsiveness may have been both a projection of the white male's sexual desires and a means of assuaging guilt over illicit, exploitative activities. Similarly, the attribution of lust to black males probably stems from the imputation of the white male's own sexual desires as well as from his fear of sexual retribution. The fear that black men lust after white women, which intensified during periods of slave insurrections, has endured to this day.

Although only one aspect of the culture of racism in colonial America, these attitudes about interracial sex revealingly express the colonists' fear and underlying sense of guilt about their enslavement of blacks. Such fears were further manifested in the elaborate slave codes erected to control the influx of blacks in the first half of the eighteenth century. The colonists seemed to play the role of what Jordan (1968) calls "anxious oppressors." They showed great hesitancy and ambivalence about converting slaves to Christianity, and as the religious distinction between themselves and Africans declined in importance, they tended to emphasize the African's appearance or racial characteristics in order to create a new justification for slavery.

Conflicting Beliefs in the Revolutionary Era

Until the middle of the eighteenth century, most of the opposition to slavery and to the racial attitudes supporting it came from the Quakers. Their strong sense of religious egalitarianism led them to object both to the treatment of slaves and to the concept of hereditary, lifetime servitude. Then, during the 1750s, two Quaker writers, Anthony Benezet and John

Woolman, led an intensified attack that condemned slavery
not only because of its negative effects on the enslaved but
also because of its corrupting influence on whites.

These views rapidly became commonplace in the revolutionary era, as abolitionists began to invoke the environmentalist theory of human differences and the natural-rights philosophy to support the antislavery position. The former mode
of thought held that human nature is the same everywhere,
although its specified character is shaped by environmental
forces. The discreditable qualities of blacks in America, such
as their purported ignorance and immorality, were due to their
enslavement. Social conditions in Africa were traceable to climate and natural environment. The most prevalent and influential abolitionist argument, however, was the inconsistency
between slavery and the revolutionary principle of the natural
right of all humans to freedom.

Defenders of slavery contended that emancipation would
violate another basic natural right for which the Revolution
had been fought—the right to private property. So sacred was
this claim that, in order not to deprive slaveholders of their
property, all but three of the Northern states that eventually
abolished slavery adopted programs allowing for the gradual
emancipation of future generations of blacks. Immediate emancipation was also deemed inappropriate because the present
generation of slaves were thought to be unfit for freedom and
unable to support themselves. Finally, there were widespread
fears that freeing slaves would inevitably lead to increased
miscegenation and outright revolt against whites (see Zilversmit, 1967).

These objections assuredly rationalized a capital investment
in slavery, but an equally important impediment to abolition
was the deep-rooted prejudice toward blacks that existed
throughout the colonies. Although protestations against slavery were common, the protesters rarely challenged the assumption of black inferiority. Indeed, the most popular abolitionist spokesman of the time, Thomas Jefferson, detested
slavery because it violated natural law, but suggested that
blacks may be biologically inferior to whites and argued that
natural differences between the groups produced inevitable

and permanent white prejudice that would not allow blacks to be incorporated into white society on equal terms. The only practical program of freedom he could envision was the colonization of blacks in Africa or the West. The same proposal was justified by later colonizationists on the basis that the inferiority of blacks was not inherent, but that white racial bias was (Fredrickson, 1971a). In either case, the idea of colonization stemmed from an underlying intolerance of blacks that precluded any thought of assimilation.

Although limited, the antislavery campaign was not completely ineffectual. Due largely to abolitionist efforts, much of the gross maltreatment of slaves was eliminated, the importation of slaves was prohibited, and slavery was abolished in the North. Still, the congressional act that ended the slave trade in 1808 marks the effective closing of the first phase of antislavery attacks. By that time the sectional division that had been developing for over a century was well defined. While gradual emancipation was underway in every state north of Maryland, the South was hardening its proslavery position and imposing greater restraints on free blacks.[4]

By the early 1800s, then, the schism between the North and the South was becoming evident. While the North could not reconcile the practice of slavery with the revolutionary ideology, the South saw the "peculiar institution" as an economic necessity. Still, almost all whites accepted the notion of black inferiority. In the North, the acceptance of black inferiority was to justify exclusion and racial discrimination following the demise of slavery, as we will see in later chapters. The important shifts in racial beliefs during the antebellum period grew out of the ideological battles between those attacking and those defending slavery.

Ideological Racism in the Antebellum Period

After a lull in the slavery debate, proslavery advocates were awakened in the 1820s by the resurgence of the colonizationist movement and the fight over the admission of Missouri to the Union. The earliest responses to these events were traditional, with southerners apologetic about the social and economic necessity of maintaining their political evil and defending slavery in Congress on legalistic and constitutional grounds. For example, the argument of states' rights was used to oppose a federally subsidized colonization program. Toward the end of the 1820s, however, proslavery expression began to take on a more aggressive, self-righteous tone that forebode a particularly virulent form of ideological racism.

The South's elaborate new defense of slavery was sparked by the rebirth of the abolitionist movement in the North. Unlike the calm, calculating opposition to slavery offered by the colonizationists, northern abolitionists like William Lloyd Garrison attacked slavery with a religious fervor. Morally outraged, they regarded slavery as an individual sin, demanded immediate freedom for slaves, and denied that racial prejudice could not be eradicated. In response to this assault, proslavery advocates developed over the next three decades an intellectual defense that held that slavery was not a "necessary evil" but a "positive good."

The Case for White Supremacy

The organizing principle and rationale of this proslavery doctrine was the permanent, biologically rooted inferiority of blacks. This was not a novel assertion at the time, but it lacked intellectual respectability prior to the 1830s and had rarely been presented by articulate whites as a philosophical defense of slavery. Earlier assumptions of inferiority had coexisted with an egalitarian philosophy by emphasizing the environmental basis of the black's inferior character and culture, while recognizing that all humans had been created equal. In the wake of the abolitionist attack, however, proslavery apologists brought "previously unarticulated assumptions" of white superiority "to the level of defensive ideological consciousness" (Fredrickson, 1971a:48).

The assumption of black inferiority appeared in different guises during this period, but the view that predominated defined the South as a *Herrenvolk* democracy, in which democracy is reserved for the master race and tyranny for subordinated groups (Fredrickson, 1971a).[5] According to slavery apologists, the inherent inferiority of blacks made them unfit for freedom and ideally suited to perpetual slavery. In support of this contention, a stereotype evolved that depicted slaves as happy, contented, and respectfully obedient to their enlightened, humane masters. Blacks were said to be better off in slavery than they had been in Africa, where, freed, they degenerated to their naturally savage natures. Such notions countered the abolitionist image of the wretched slave, assured southerners that slavery was moral, and assured slavemasters fearful of rebellion that their slaves were controlled and contented (Fredrickson, 1971a; Takaki, 1970).

The case for slavery and white supremacy became an absorbing interest of southerners during this period. Drawing upon evidence from a wide variety of sources, proslavery propagandists argued the case in books, newspapers, periodicals, sermons, and lectures (see Jenkins, 1935). Traditional arguments were refined and voiced with renewed vigor. The historical case against blacks was that they had failed to develop a civilized way of life in Africa. The biblical story of the curse on Canaan was a popular justification of their relegation to slavery, as was the old contention that abolition would lead to widespread miscegenation and the degeneration of the white race. Biological arguments were also advanced, particularly the physiological and anatomical basis of black inferiority. However, although the accepted opinion in scientific circles in the 1840s and 1850s was that blacks were a separate and unequal species, this opinion was probably peripheral to the defense of slavery. Ethnological theories were beyond most laymen; they conflicted with orthodox religious beliefs; and, in general, they were not politicized by American scientists (Stanton, 1960).

Abolitionists' Attitudes

Abolitionists, rather than basing their case on moral and intellectual equality, acknowledged vast racial differences and developed a distinctive conception of the black character. These "romantic racialists," as Fredrickson (1971a) describes them, essentially interpreted differently the "childlike simplicity" image of slaves promulgated by proslavery paternalists. Whereas the latter saw the qualities of meekness, tran-

quility, affection, and loyalty as evidence of blacks' suitability
and adaptability to slavery, the abolitionists contended that
these attributes exemplified the highest Christian virtues. The
novel *Uncle Tom's Cabin* did much to popularize this benign
image, depicting the blacks' proclivity to gentleness, affection,
and forgiveness in the character of Uncle Tom. However, in
spite of this glorification of blacks' superior aptitude for Christianity, the romantic racialists' acknowledgement of permanent racial differences, especially the greater energy and intellectual superiority of whites, weakened their moral
objections to slavery and to other forms of racial discrimination. Although abolitionists of this stripe were active and articulate, their demands for immediate emancipation and equal
treatment of free blacks never won wide acceptance north or
south of the Mason-Dixon line.

Abolitionists who demanded complete equality constituted
a small "radical" minority in the antislavery coalition of the
1840s and 1850s. The majority were white nationalists who
believed in manifest destiny and the desirability of a racially
homogeneous society.[6] This segment was motivated by practical and political aims rather than moral repulsion to racial
oppression. They were both antislavery and antiblack. A few
managed to uphold equal rights for blacks, but most did not
support legal or social equality. Concerned about racial purity
and the competition of black labor in the western states and
territories, white nationalists simultaneously demanded the
prohibition of slavery and the exclusion of free Negroes from
these areas (see Berwanger, 1967). They also anxiously endorsed the idea of repatriation, which once again became popular in the 1850s.[7]

Abraham Lincoln himself reflected the public mind on questions of race. Indeed, as Litwack (1961:276) notes, Lincoln's
"nomination and election would have been problematical" if
he had not vehemently opposed the expansion of slavery. He
also went to great lengths to deny political opponents' claims
that he favored full political and social equality for blacks.
And, at the dawn of the Civil War, he believed that colonization offered the only hope of solving the racial problem.

In the same manner that southerners rationalized the inconsistency between slavery and democratic principles, northerners maintained that their own system of racial segregation and discrimination was simply the inevitable consequence of blacks' natural inferiority. Because the forms of racial oppression practiced in the North were comparatively less offensive than the institution of southern slavery, the hard-core ideological defenses constructed by southern slaveholders were not required in the North. Still, scientific and biblical explanations of blacks' subordination were widely accepted in the North, with the threat of racial amalgamation frequently justifying segregation, particularly in the schools. These beliefs were further buttressed by a wide range of negative images of blacks popularized by the press, by black minstrels, and by politicians pandering to insecure whites. The stereotype that emerged characterized blacks as clownish, immature, lazy, immoral, and ignorant. As always, such racist beliefs interacted with repressive discrimination and segregation, each shaping and reinforcing the other. Thus, antiblack attitudes gave rise to and supported oppressive discrimination that, by reducing the condition of blacks to poverty and illiteracy, reinforced the same attitudes.

The Civil War and After

By the dawn of the Civil War, then, the belief in the inherent inferiority of blacks was widely accepted, even among radical abolitionists, and was the premise for thought and action toward blacks in both the North and the South. The early "bestial" assumptions had been tempered, but the presumption of black inferiority had been supplemented by an equally damaging set of beliefs. As biologically inferior beings, blacks were said to evidence a gentle, childlike immaturity, clownishness, and laziness that made it impossible for them to participate in white society. As we will see in later chapters, these more "benign" beliefs were to be as damaging as earlier "bestial" conceptions. Indeed, they were to justify forms of racial oppression amounting to the civil enslavement of blacks long after slavery was legally abolished, for if blacks are "Samboish," they must be excluded from "adult" white society. And so, whether used to justify Jim Crow laws, deportation schemes, or outright acts of discrimination, beliefs about black inferiority were to shape the institutionalization of discrimination against blacks in the latter half of the nineteenth century.

Although the Civil War brought about the demise of slavery and the extension of rights to blacks throughout the states, these were not the aims of the North at the outset of the war. By 1860, only a small minority of whites still clamored for emancipation, and hardly anyone could countenance the idea of full equality for blacks. The Republican platform on which Lincoln ran opposed the extension of slavery but pledged to protect the institution where it existed. So, when war broke, the immediate aim was to preserve the Union. But as the conflict grew, slavery came to be understood as the root issue of the war. It was believed that the North and the South would be drawn into conflict again if slavery did not die with the Confederacy. The idea of a "new birth of liberty" also evolved, providing northerners with "an unclouded vision of the war that could engage their feelings and profoundest ideals" (Kincaid, 1970:53). Such beliefs paved the way for the Emancipation Proclamation and subsequently for the Thirteenth Amendment, which permanently abolished slavery throughout the Union.

Racial Extremism in the
Post-Civil War Period

The nationalism that spurred the abolition of slavery fell far short of eliminating the strong sense of racial difference that existed before the war. National unity and progress were widely associated with racial homogeneity, and even the most liberal racial thinkers were generally unwilling to regard blacks as anything more than "temporary and inferior sojourners in a white America" (Fredrickson, 1971a:164). After emancipation, such assumptions fostered some fantastic speculations about the future of blacks in America, many of which predicted their disappearance. A few race theorists foretold the extinction of blacks as a result of "natural processes," contending that though the black population had increased in slavery, inherited weaknesses would put blacks at a disadvantage in competition with whites. Lincoln himself made several abortive attempts to establish black colonies abroad. Moreover, northern fears of a massive northern migration of ex-slaves following emancipation were allayed by the assertion that ex-slaves would remain in the South where the climate was more congenial to them.

Emancipation and Reconstruction actually did nothing to change the caste status of southern blacks for, as we will see in the next chapter, black laborers were as dependent upon white employers as slaves had been. Whites comprised a substantial majority of the population in all but three states, and they possessed nearly all of the money, land, education, social prestige, and political experience. Without a full-scale social and economic revolution, therefore, it was inevitable that white southerners would eventually control the destiny of the South. And since the South was vehemently opposed to black equality, northern protection was essential to preserve the newly acquired rights of blacks. During the period of Radical Reconstruction, the North stationed troops in the South to enforce these rights. But in 1877, when its own ends were no longer served by protecting black suffrage, the North abandoned the South and left the freedmen to shift for themselves.[8]

Consequences of Radical Reconstruction

Northern abandonment of the South was rationalized by a set of beliefs that were not intrinsically racist but nonetheless had racist consequences. The conception of egalitarianism accepted at this time, "equality before the law," was thought to be compatible with vast disparities in the wealth and power of individuals or groups. Consistent with this concept was the dominant laissez-faire ideology which assumed that equal rights produced equal opportunities and that no group should be extended special favors not available to others. On the basis of such beliefs, even the staunchest promoters of the cause of black rights felt that blacks must make it on their own once they were extended basic rights. But this very idea suggests that blacks as a group were to find their social niche rather than being fully integrated individually up and down the social ladder (Fredrickson, 1971a:179). Moreover, the fact that blacks entered Reconstruction at a severe competitive disadvantage did not seriously challenge the "equal opportunity" doctrine, because the failure of blacks was predicted by the prevailing belief in black racial inferiority. Thus, by 1877, after the rumor of corruption and misgovernment in black Reconstruction regimes had thoroughly circulated in the North, most Americans were willing to believe that blacks had been "given their fair chance" and hence deserved their inferior status (see Fredrickson, 1971a:175-86).

In the South, Radical Reconstruction had even worse consequences for blacks, ultimately fostering the most extreme form of "Negrophobia" yet witnessed in America. Several factors contributed to the ruthless resubjugation of blacks (Kincaid, 1970). First, blacks became the objects of the hatred and frustration that defeated white southerners felt toward the North. Blacks were regularly blamed for every imaginable southern ill, from the corruption of Reconstruction governments (blacks being intellectually inferior and susceptible to demagoguery) to the failure of southern agriculture (black labor being inefficient). The sudden collapse of the old social order with its traditional restraints on black people also rekindled racial fears and prejudices. After two hundred years of slavery, laws could not undo the southern image of black "child-savages" who, without the control of slavery, threatened the lives of white people and the values of southern civilization. Southern whites—anxious at the thought of blacks as free citizens who could vote, hold office, own land, and work for themselves—sought to reaffirm their supremacy through new forms of racial subordination. Finally, political competition between blacks and whites had two unfortunate effects: (1) it provided fuel to southern fire-eating politicians who found racist appeals potent weapons in political contests, and (2) it led supporters of the Confederacy who were denied the right to vote during Radical Reconstruction to resort to extralegal means to intimidate blacks, especially black voters and officeholders.

The Rise of Jim Crow

The new structure of white dominance erected by the South following Reconstruction consisted of the social and economic separation of the races. As this system evolved in the late nineteenth century, it was rationalized by a doctrine of white supremacy that differed from the proslavery argument mainly in a new undisguised hatred of blacks. The theme of the loyal and devoted black who must be benevolently guided by whites, which had been portrayed by many antebellum propagandists for slavery, was abandoned and formed no part of the new segregationist dogma. According to this doctrine (see Guion Johnson, 1949):

1. Whether it be from racial prejudice or racial pride, racial segregation is natural and instinctive in human nature. It is desired by both races and for the good of both.
2. Political power should remain in the hands of whites since they possess the superior intelligence and wealth. Moreover, blacks should not be granted suffrage because they are incapable of intelligently exercising this right.
3. Blacks are permanently inferior beings necessitating segregation to control inherent criminality and inordinate sexual passions. Social equality encourages oversexed black males to violate white women.
4. Segregation also guards against racial amalgamation or intermarriage, which is sinful, unnatural, and begets hybrid monstrosities.

In the 1890s, following a generation in which blacks had been tolerated as voters in most parts of the South, the most extreme racism occurred. As a result of the decline in southern agriculture for which blacks were made the scapegoat, and of the political successes of southern conservative extremists in the face of fading northern opposition, the South completely disenfranchised blacks, legally codified its system of racial segregation, and increasingly resorted to lynching and other brutalities to keep blacks in their place (Woodward, 1966; Gossett, 1963). Racist beliefs also reached the nadir, perhaps in part to remove "the intolerable burden of guilt for perpetrating or tolerating the most horrendous cruelties and injustices" (Fredrickson, 1971a:282). One popular view held that blacks had degenerated as freedmen. Without the compulsion and supervision of slavery, and under the competitive pressures of "freedom," blacks were said to have retrogressed to their natural state, in which they are lazy, shiftless, and licentious. Lynching was similarly defended as an "unfortunate" practice brought about by the black man's own beastly and brutal nature. Such beliefs originated in the proslavery conception of blacks as having a dual nature—childlike and docile when enslaved, but savage and criminal when free. The white racist imagination at the turn of the century differed from the antebellum southern mind only in its full-blown, unrestrained expression.[9]

Social Darwinism

Providing a powerful rationale for racist beliefs and practices during the late nineteenth century was a theory of societal progress called "Social Darwinism." The Darwinian theory of evolution became translated into the notion of "evolving" groups and societies. The idea of varieties and species progressing to higher forms of life through a competitive process of natural selection was applied to the struggle between individual members of society and between different human groups. When applied to different races, the "survival of the fittest" could mean only the superior white race. And since the biological struggle for existence was nature's indispensable method for human progress, races should be left free to compete for the limited resources. The "failure" of blacks during Reconstruction, after northern intervention on their behalf, "demonstrated" the futility of interfering with the natural forces of evolution. And if blacks were a degenerating race with no future, as many racial Darwinists predicted, the urgent need was to segregate them in order not to endanger or contaminate the white race (see Fredrickson, 1971a:ch. 8; Gossett, 1963:ch. 7).

Social Darwinism came under attack around the turn of the century by social reformers and social scientists who, reacting in part to the excesses of southern racism, rejected the idea of inevitable conflict and competition within society and argued for social progress based on regulation and cooperation. Such views won wide acceptance among northern progressives. However, because this group did not challenge some of the most basic racist assumptions, they had little restraining influence on racial extremism in the South and little effect upon the development of "scientific" racism. Many of these "moderate" racists accepted the permanent inferiority of blacks, and most maintained that racial purity and integrity as well as an instinct of race prejudice demanded racial segregation.

The essence of their argument for tolerant benevolence was that blacks, as a "child race," were naturally docile and kindly and could become useful, peaceful citizens through white guidance and self-help. Since the "Negro race" was less advanced on the evolutionary scale than the white, the "wheels of progress" needed to be oiled by providing education, industrial training, and moral uplift. As we will observe in chapters 4 and 5, the model for racial moderates was Booker T. Washington, founder of the Tuskegee Institute, who advocated self-help, industrial education, and black accommodation to racial segregation.

Science and Twentieth-Century Racial Beliefs

Entering the twentieth century, Americans were probably less disposed to accept the social equality of blacks than at any other period in their history. Racist thought was respectable among all social classes and in all sections of the country. The South, defending its efforts to disenfranchise and legally segregate blacks, was inundating the nation with a mass of anti-Negro literature. The North, concerned with the nation's imperialistic ventures and channeling its reformist energies into other areas,[10] mounted no serious challenge to southern race policies. Finally, American interest in "scientific" racism blossomed after 1900, receiving wide attention from those who, in the burgeoning age of science, felt compelled to give their ideas an elaborate scientific rationale. As a result, during the first quarter of the century, sociologists, psychologists, and biologists developed a comprehensive science of race that firmly affixed upon blacks a stigma of inferiority more damaging and more humiliating in many respects than that of slavery (Newby, 1965:21). To this day, blacks still suffer from that stigma.

Racism in Science

The source of racism in biology was the newly developing fields of genetics and eugenics. Darwin's theories had convinced biologists that evolution accounted for race differences and hence for racial inequality. It remained for the science of heredity to explain the mechanisms underlying the evolution of these differences. Experiments with plant genetics and hybridization were believed to demonstrate the overwhelming importance of heredity in the transmission of human characteristics, supporting the notion of innate black inferiority. Eugenicists warned that racial intermixture led to biological abnormalities, and urged the adoption of public policies that would curtail the birthrate of undesirable races such as Negroes. Even biologists who did not accept the theory of racial "abnormalities" sometimes deplored race intermixture, reasoning that crosses between inferior and superior races must produce offspring intermediate between the two parent groups (Gossett, 1963).

In psychology, a parallel development in the assessment of mental and emotional differences between the races was also thought to support the assumption of the black's innate inferiority. Intelligence testing, which originated in France in 1905 and developed rapidly in the following decade, was applied on a massive scale to men coming into the armed services after American entry into World War I. The tests, particularly the "army beta" test designed for illiterates and immigrants unfamiliar with English, were claimed to be objective measures of innate intellectual ability. Consequently, when blacks' scores turned out to be lower than whites' on the average, a powerful tool was placed in the hands of racists who would argue that the racial inferiority of blacks was an established scientific fact.

Sociologists also contributed, often unwittingly, to the body of scientific knowledge upon which racists drew at this time. For example, the famous University of Chicago sociologist William I. Thomas (1904:610) maintained that race prejudice was "an instinct originating in the tribal stage of society, when solidarity in feeling and action were essential to the preservation of the group," and that it would "probably never disappear completely." Others lent support to the notion of instinctive intergroup antipathy by arguing that the vast physical and psychical differences between the races fostered a "caste feeling" and "consciousness of kind" that was strongest among the "superior" white race. Finally, Robert Park, a sociological authority on race relations in the period between the wars, celebrated black artistic achievements during the "Harlem Renaissance" of the 1920s as an expression of the black's superior emotionalism and sensuality, thus confirming part of the traditional stereotype of blacks as "expressive" and "sensual."

During the first quarter of the twentieth century, then, reputable scientists in several fields furnished an abundance of authoritative "proof" of black inferiority and instinctive racial antipathy. Although many of these scientists maintained a purely academic interest in the subject of race and argued against the use of their ideas to justify discriminatory policies toward blacks, their ideas nonetheless became the foundation of sophisticated defenses of segregation and social inequality. Popular writers such as Lothrop Stoddard, who felt that as a "scientific humanist" he was morally obligated to warn the nation about the perils of race, made the "new 'truths' of science concerning race available to great numbers of people" (Gossett, 1963:390). Against the backdrop of the events of this period, these "truths" gained heightened significance.

The Great Migration

The mass migration of southern blacks to the North during World War I had a great impact on racial attitudes toward blacks. This movement caused deep resentment among working-class people with whom blacks competed for jobs. The result was the outbreak of several race riots in 1919 and the surfacing of racial prejudices. The great wave of foreign immigration in the late nineteenth and early twentieth centuries also raised concern over race, making restrictive immigration legislation the chief political objective of racists in the 1920s and inviting the usual invidious comparisons between white and black races. In the end, such events were to make the problem of black-white relations national in scope and to cause reflective people in the sciences to question the scientific truths to which racists appealed.

A New Attitude

The scientific backing that racists had received was finally revoked in the 1920s and 1930s. Throughout the history of the United States, there had always been a few whites who were able to see through the illogic and irrationality of racism; but not until the anthropologist Franz Boas led the attack in the 1920s did the opponents of racism gain a sizable following. Boas forcefully exposed the mass of contradictory evidence, errors of judgment, and faulty generalizations associated with studies of race. At the same time, he offered a well-reasoned cultural explanation of why races all over the world reveal diversity. Engaged in the study of aboriginal peoples, Boas argued that the intelligence and temperament of individuals are not associated with the racial inheritance of bodily characteristics and could only be meaningfully interpreted in terms of the language, beliefs, and customs of their culture. Boas was also highly critical of the assumption of inferiority and superiority among races or cultures and of the failure of scientists to dissociate their judgments from the standards of their own culture, a criticism that psychologists soon applied to intelligence tests.

By the late 1920s, the tide had turned against racism in all the sciences. Psychologists disclosed the biases inherent in mental tests. Careful analysis of the results of these tests clearly demonstrated the powerful effect of the environment, leading to the conclusion that there is no evidence of inherent racial differences in intelligence. Among biologists, arguments against the harmful effects of miscegenation gained force, as did the idea that both heredity and environment collectively determine the traits of an organism. In a similar vein, sociologists shifted their emphasis from the biological and instinctive basis of human relationships to one based upon social and cultural factors, with the result that racial prejudice was no longer understood as an innate aversion but as a consequence of social forces (see Gossett, 1963:ch. 16; Rose, 1968).

From these scientific developments there emerged a new enlightened perspective in white racial thinking that Fredrickson (1971a) has labeled "liberal environmentalism." The major tenet of this view is that all apparent social, cultural, and intellectual differences between the races are the product of environment. Hence, blacks are seen as the products of an oppressive environment that creates discontent, frustration, and a sense of powerlessness. By World War II such thinking completely dominated the fields of sociology and anthropology and was becoming increasingly influential among the liberal public.

Adding force to this perspective was the growth of socialist thinking, which recognized the harmful effects of economic and social deprivation. Further, the emergence of black political power as evidenced by the shift of black voters to the Democratic party in the election of 1936 and the threatened march on Washington in 1942 began to awaken the public to the oppression of blacks. During World War II, when the horrors of Nazi racism were revealed and the democratic-egalitarian ideology of the "American creed" was once again called forth, the liberal environmentalist doctrine finally triumphed as the respectable thought in intellectual and academic circles.

The importance of this triumph for race relations in America is inestimable. The new egalitarian doctrine provided the theoretical basis of the civil rights movement of the 1950s and 1960s and was influential in the legislative and court decisions that this movement produced. It offered the first serious challenge to the most fundamental racist belief in America—that blacks are inherently inferior to whites. Although millions of Americans still associate race with character, intelligence, and human worth, blatant racist beliefs are no longer respectable, and today only a small segment of the population will publicly acknowledge a belief in black intellectual inferiority. Perhaps of even greater ultimate significance, the thorough debunking of racial theories of human differences has meant that racists have found it increasingly difficult to invoke the authority of science to support their views.[11]

Present and Future Beliefs

Thus far, the works of historians have been drawn upon to present a panoramic view of changes in white racial beliefs over a three-hundred-year period. The historians themselves relied upon secondary analyses of newspapers, printed speeches, letters, and similar materials. With the advent of public opinion polling in the late 1930s, however, a different kind of record emerged for documenting racial beliefs and attitudes. An examination of this record not only reveals the substance of contemporary beliefs but also suggests future trends.

While the foregoing historical overview has shown some distinctive shifts in racial beliefs over time, until the middle of this century the overwhelming majority of whites accepted a doctrine of white supremacy. This doctrine included a stereotype of blacks as inherently inferior to whites in fundamental qualities such as intelligence, ambition, and temperament. Such differences were thought to be permanent and were used, in turn, to justify opposition to racial integration, especially in the form of intermarriage.

The opinions of white Americans toward black Americans with respect to racial differences and acceptance of black-white integration have been polled repeatedly since the early 1940s. According to these polls, what changes, if any, have occurred?

Contemporary Attitudes towards Blacks

At the beginning of the chapter, we noted that in 1942 only 42 percent of a nationwide sample of whites said they believed that "Negroes are as intelligent as white people . . . if they are given the same education and training." This is a very important belief, for it is central to the white image of black inferiority. When the National Opinion Research Center (NORC) asked the same question in subsequent national surveys, the percentage increased to 53 percent in 1946 and then to 77 percent in 1956 before dipping slightly to 76 percent in 1963 (Hyman and Sheatsley, 1964). The question has not been included in NORC surveys since 1963. However, Louis Harris and Associates (see Williams, Buckley, and Lord, 1979) have addressed the same issue throughout the 1960s and 1970s with a differently worded question. In this case, respondents were asked whether they personally tended to agree or disagree that "blacks have less native intelligence than whites," a statement, respondents were told, that "people sometimes make about black people." Apparently because of the different way the question was asked, the responses to the Harris survey were less "liberal" than responses to the NORC polls of 1956 and 1963. Still, the percentage of people who disagreed with the Harris statement rose from 61 percent in 1963 to 75 percent in 1978 (see table 2.1). Thus, the two sets of polling results together show a substantial decline between 1942 and 1978 in a publicly stated belief that is central to the inherent-inequality doctrine.

During the period 1963 to 1978, the Harris polls also asked national samples about their willingness to endorse several other statements reflecting stereotyped beliefs about blacks. The results of these surveys are summarized in table 2.1. These data show a general decline in the number of whites holding to the traditional black stereotype. On the other hand, the higher percentages in 1967, a year of major urban unrest, suggest that this more positive image can be altered by racial events; therefore, it would not appear to be deeply ingrained. Furthermore, a substantial number of whites still subscribe to invidious stereotypes. For example, 49 percent agree with the statement, "Blacks tend to have less ambition than whites." The overall picture, then, is one of a general decline in racial stereotyping, but of a sizeable minority who still hold a negative image of blacks.

Attitudes toward Integration

The pattern of changes in attitudes toward integration appears, on the surface, to be more favorable. In 1942, and then beginning in 1956 at seven-year intervals, the National Opin-

TABLE 2.1.

Percentage of white respondents who agree with stereotyped statements about blacks 1963–1978.

Statement	1963	1966	1967	1971	1976	1978
Blacks tend to have less ambition than whites	66	65	70	52	50	49
Blacks want to live off the handout	41	43	52	39	37	36
Blacks are more violent than whites	*	*	42	36	35	34
Blacks breed crime	35	33	32	27	31	29
Blacks have less native intelligence than whites	39	36	46	37	28	25
Blacks care less for the family than whites	31	33	34	26	22	18
Blacks are inferior to white people	31	26	29	22	15	15

* Question not asked.

Source: From "A New Racial Poll" by D.A. Williams, J. Buckley and M. Lord, Newsweek (Feb. 26, 1979): 48, 53.

ion Research Center asked national samples of whites a series of questions about racial integration (Hyman and Sheatsley, 1964; Sheatsley, 1966; Greeley and Sheatsley, 1971; Taylor, Sheatsley, and Greeley, 1978; Condran, 1979). Table 2.2 presents some results from these surveys. The trend in all areas is toward increased tolerance of racial integration. The earliest pro-integration shifts occurred in less personal areas such as

TABLE 2.2.

Percentage of respondents giving pro-integration responses to questions about integration, 1942–1977.

Question*	1942	1956	1963	1970	1977
Transportation	44	60	77	88	†
Schools	30	48	63	72	86
Neighborhood(a)	35	51	64	85('72)	†
Neighborhood(b)	†	†	44	50	58
Dinner	†	†	49	62	71
Marriage	†	†	36	49	72

Transportation: "Generally speaking, do you think there should be separate sections for Negroes in streetcars and buses?" ("No.")

Schools: "Do you think white students and Negro (black) students should go to the same schools or to separate schools?" ("Same schools.")

Neighborhood(a): "If a Negro with the same income and education as you have, moved into your block, would it make any difference to you?" ("No difference.")

Neighborhood(b): "White people have a right to keep Negroes (blacks) out of their neighborhoods if they want to, and Negroes (blacks) should respect that right." ("Disagree slightly" or "Disagree strongly.")

Dinner: "How strongly would you object if a member of your family wanted to bring a Negro (black) friend home to dinner? ("Not at all object.")

Marriage: "Do you think there should be laws against marriages between Negroes (blacks) and whites?" ("No.")

† Question not asked.

Source: National Opinion Research Center

transportation, but by the late 1970s, a majority of whites expressed tolerance for invitations to one's home and intermarriage. The NORC surveys have consistently found greater tolerance among whites who are younger or well educated or living in the North. Still, the same basic trend is found in all age cohorts, all educational strata, and all regions. Since World War II, then, the polls indicate a steady increase in white public acceptance of racial integration, to the point where, entering the 1980s, pro-integration attitudes represented the dominant position in America, even in the South.

Public versus Private Beliefs

At the same time, there is reason to question the depth of these changes in beliefs and attitudes. For one thing, such surveys may be more a measure of what people are willing to say publicly than of what they really feel. White Americans simply may have "improved their conformity to the increasingly institutionalized normative standards of an officially 'liberal' society" (Condran, 1979:474). In fact, there is evidence of indirect resistance and incomplete acceptance of racial integration among those who publicly appear tolerant.

For example, while the polling data show that whites have become much more willing to accept black neighbors (see table 2.2), continuing residential segregation seems to be largely a matter of white preference for segregated neighborhoods. When a Detroit area survey (Farley, et al., 1978) presented white respondents with diagrams of a variety of neighborhoods, a majority said they were not willing to move into a nice, affordable house in a neighborhood that is 20 percent black, and three quarters were unwilling to move to a neighborhood that is 33 percent black. On the other hand, there was widespread acceptance of residential integration on the usual indicators such as willingness to sell to a black or to have a "black on your block." Thus, when the question went beyond abstract values and moved toward how respondents personally felt in specific situations, whites were much less tolerant.

A similar pattern exists with respect to racial integration in the schools. In contrast to support for the principle of integrated schools, the number of whites opposed to having their child attend a school where the majority of pupils are blacks actually increased in the 1970s after a period of decline in the 1960s (Simon, 1974; Davis, 1978). Closely related, upwards of 80 percent of whites have remained strongly opposed, throughout the 1970s, to the busing of white school children from one district to another (Davis, 1978), usually the only realistic method for achieving school integration.

In contrast to the sanguine polling results showing a reduction in white opposition to formal racial equality, then, these responses suggest that white racism has far from disappeared. Rather, there appears to have been a shift in the manifest content of white racism coincident with the change in racial policy issues in the late 1960s (Kinder and Sears, 1981). With the passage of civil rights legislation in the 1960s and explicit legal discrimination no longer at issue, the struggle for racial progress became concentrated on "forcing" institutions to be actively egalitarian. The symbols of this shift in policy—affirmative action, busing, and racial quotas—have become the focus of what has been called "symbolic racism" (Sears, Hensler, and Speer, 1979; Kinder and Sears, 1981). According to Kinder and Sears' (1981:416) formulation, this style of racism combines antiblack anxiety and hostility with traditional American moral values such as individualism and self-reliance. Placing their faith in the Protestant work ethic, whites have become indignant over the sense that blacks are playing by a different and easier set of rules as a result of "unfair" government assistance. Symbolic racism therefore finds its clearest expression on such issues as: welfare ("welfare cheats could find work if they tried"); affirmative action ("blacks should not be given a status they have not earned"); busing ("whites have worked hard for their . . . neighborhood schools"); and "free" abortions for the poor ("if blacks behaved morally, they would not need abortions").

Ample evidence exists that something akin to symbolic racism is the dominant form of racial beliefs in American society today. As we noted earlier, a vast majority of whites continue to express antiblack sentiments on the symbolic issue of busing for racial integration. Kinder and Sears (1981) found similar strong opposition to quotas for black college students, as well as widespread beliefs that blacks get more than they deserve and that blacks on welfare could get along without it if they tried. Moreover, national polls throughout the 1970s and early 1980s consistently showed that though most Americans favored equal rights and equal opportunity, they overwhelmingly rejected any form of "forced" integration and preferential treatment (Lipset and Schneider, 1978). In recent years, over 70 percent of the American public has endorsed the statement, "Blacks shouldn't push themselves where they are not wanted" (Davis, 1978). A majority of whites have been disturbed by the pace of change in race relations. Finally, whites have generally favored "integration in some areas of life" over "full racial integration" and have said that they would feel "uneasy" if a close relative were planning to marry someone of another race (Lipset and Schneider, 1978). In short, while Americans support racial equality, they have been slow to accept full racial integration; they tend to resent efforts to force it on them; and they are concerned about programs that violate the values of individual freedom and fair individual competition.

Kinder and Sears (1981) found that their own measures of symbolic racism were unrelated to whites' current social status or to direct racial threats to whites' private lives such as neighborhood desegregation and the likelihood of having a child bused to achieve school desegregation. This latest version of white racism has less to do with the current realities of whites' lives than with racial attitudes and moral values learned years ago. To the extent that this accurately characterizes contemporary beliefs, it simply reflects the latent racial hostility that over three hundred fifty years of racism has imbued in American culture. And as long as this hostility persists, it will threaten America's commitment to racial equality.

The Sociocultural Dynamics of Oppression

In this chapter, we have sought to summarize the beliefs that have been used to legitimate discriminatory practices against black Americans. As we stressed in the last chapter, oppression can only occur when discriminatory acts become institutionalized—that is, when they are built into social structures and legitimated by cultural beliefs and legal codes. For even if a population is distinguishable, powerless, and threatening (the other conditions of oppression), it will be difficult to oppress this population in the long run without institutionalization.

The beliefs outlined in this chapter have been critical in the oppression of blacks. But they are only the cultural component of oppression. We now need to examine in more detail the social structural arrangements that these beliefs have legitimated. In particular, we should focus on those social structures that are most critical in influencing people's life-chances— economy, government, law, and education.

As we review the history of discrimination in these structural spheres, we should recall the cultural beliefs outlined in this chapter. It is these beliefs that have made economic, political, educational, and legal discrimination seem "right and proper" or, at the very least, "acceptable." After this review of social structural oppression, we will attempt to outline in a more precise manner the interplay between the cultural beliefs discussed in this chapter and the social structural arrangements examined in the next four chapters. It is in this interplay that the unique character of oppression of black Americans resides.

CHAPTER THREE

Economic Oppression

The interplay between cultural beliefs and social structural arrangements is complex. On the one hand, structural arrangements require cultural legitimation, while on the other hand, emerging cultural beliefs set limits on which social arrangements are seen as desirable and possible. The history of white oppression of blacks has thus seen a complex interplay between the cultural beliefs outlined in the last chapter and the social structural arrangements to be delineated in this and the next chapters. Whether cultural beliefs "cause" structures of oppression, or vice versa, is less critical than the recognition that prejudicial beliefs and discriminatory structures constitute a system. As such, their power to control the access of an oppressed population to valued resources is that much greater.

In this chapter, we begin our analysis of the structure of oppression by examining the history of black economic participation. Our goal is to show how discriminatory actions within the economic sphere have, over the long course of American history, operated to maintain blacks at the bottom ranks of the stratification system. Such discriminatory actions have been legitimated by the cultural beliefs discussed in the last chapter. Hence, reference to chapter 2 can serve to aid in

43

interpreting the economic course of events. Moreover, patterns of culturally legitimated economic oppression have been supported and reinforced in other institutional arrangements—the topics of the following chapters. Examination of economic oppression thus represents only one sphere of a complex system of institutionalized oppression.

Early Forms of Economic Oppression

Prior to the Civil War (1861–1865), the economy of the South had become heavily dependent upon a large black slave population. While the historical record is vague on just when slavery was first institutionalized, it is clear that by 1670 most American blacks found themselves and their offspring forced into lifelong servitude. Slavery became rapidly institutionalized because of the agricultural economy of the South. In contrast to the North, which was beginning to industrialize and urbanize as early as the American Revolution (1775–1783), the South was still heavily agricultural, its economy relying on the export of cotton, tobacco, hemp, rice, wheat, and sugar. While different states tended to specialize in only some of these crops, all southern states had one feature in common: reliance upon an inexpensive and relatively large black labor pool to cultivate large tracts of land. It is not clear whether or not slavery was the most efficient form of agricultural organization (see Genovese, 1965; Fogel and Engerman, 1974), but the shortage of alternative sources of labor and the abundance of land in the southern colonies placed a high value on involuntary labor. As a result, slaves were used to initiate the plantation system and, once initiated, the system encouraged increased importation of slaves in all southern states.

There is considerable disagreement, even among authoritative sources, as to exactly how many slaves were imported to this country. Yet, blacks constituted a large percentage of the total population, particularly in the South. Official census figures must be read with caution because they probably underestimate the black population.[1] Nevertheless, the official government data report a heavy concentration of black labor in the agrarian South. As shown in table 3.1, the southern population was 35 percent black in 1790, and remained at this level until after the Civil War. Moreover, blacks were most heavily concentrated in the Deep South (from South Carolina to Louisiana), where over 40 percent of the total population was slave (Wesley, 1927:9).

TABLE 3.1.

Blacks as a percentage of the total population, 1790–1980.

Year	United States	South	North	West
1790	19	35	3	—
1870	13	36	2	1
1910	11	30	2	1
1940	10	24	4	1
1960	11	21	7	4
1970	11	19	8	5
1975	11	19	9	6
1980	12	19	10	5

Source: U.S. Department of Commerce, Bureau of the Census, No. 80 (1979a), p. 23; Hill (1979), p. 25; and U.S. Department of Commerce, Bureau of the Census (1982), p. 22.

The pattern of southern economic dependence upon slavery becomes evident when we consider the slave-owning family. Table 3.2, which reports the geographical distribution of slaves and slave-owning families, shows the attraction of slaveholding to the South. Between 1790 and 1850, there was a sharp decline in the percentage of slave-owning families in the United States. Yet in 1850, over 40 percent of families in the five Deep South states owned slaves. By comparison, the percentage of slave-owning families in the total U.S. population was a mere 10 percent.

In the South by 1850, slave ownership involved a sizeable minority of families, dominated by a much smaller number of politically powerful, large landowners. For the most part, these large landowners raised cotton and tobacco. Cotton, however, was king, with nearly two million workers, representing 72.6 percent of the southern black labor force, employed in its production (Wesley, 1927).We begin to see the pattern of early American racial economic exploitation: large cotton and, to a lesser extent, tobacco plantations dominated southern U.S. agriculture, and these economic organizations were the primary developers and exploiters of black slave labor.

The large masses of black slaves were kept in line, economically speaking, by a small but powerful minority of large landowners. Large landowners also dictated the moral style of the nineteenth-century South. The largest 12,000 southern plantations—which comprised only 12 percent of the total—owned 50 percent of all available black slave labor in 1850; that is, they owned approximately 1.5 million of a total population of approximately 3 million black slaves.[2] Large landowners kept blacks in line by stripping them of cultural and family ties. The landowners recruited overseers for black slaves from among poor white laborers, most of whom were convinced that it was in their best interest to keep blacks in their place at the bottom rung of the southern economic ladder.

By the dawn of the Civil War, much of the southern economy had come to rely upon slave labor. It was the complete institutionalization of slavery into the southern economy, plus fear among poor southern whites of violence by oppressed blacks, that partially accounted for the resistance of that "peculiar institution" to change (Stampp, 1956). Black slaves and poor whites alike were kept in line by a prevailing belief system that dictated the pattern of exploitation and animosity between them and that served to divert their attention from the expropriation by large landowners of the economic resources of the South.

The existence of a vulnerable white labor force operated to perpetuate both the oppression of blacks in economic servitude, and the privilege of elites who profited from the labor of slaves. Indeed, the existence of a large and very inexpensive pool of black labor posed a real threat to the well-being of poor whites whose own wages could be easily undercut by free black workers. As we emphasized in chapter 1, such threat by

TABLE 3.2.

Distribution of black slaves and slaveholding families by selected divisions and states, 1790 and 1850.

Area and year	Total black slaves (thousands)	Slaveholding families		Average number of slaves per slaveholding family
		Number[1] (thousands)	Percent of all families	
1790				
UNITED STATES, TOTAL[2]	698	96	23	7.3
South Atlantic	642	77	72	8.3
Delaware	9	2[3]	(NA)	4.8
Maryland	103	14	41	7.5
District of Columbia	—	—	(NA)	—
Virginia[4]	293	34[3]	(NA)	8.5
North Carolina	101	16	33	6.7
South Carolina	107	9	34	12.1
Georgia	29	2[3]	(NA)	12.1
Florida	—	—	—	—

Table 3.2 continued on next page

47

continued from previous page

| | Total black slaves (thousands) | Slaveholding families | | Average number of slaves per slaveholding family |
Area and year		Number[1] (thousands)	Percent of all families	
East South Central	16	2	(NA)	6.7
Kentucky	12	2[3]	(NA)	6.7
Tennessee	3	1[3]	(NA)	6.7
Alabama	—	—	(NA)	—
Mississippi	—	—	(NA)	—
1850				
UNITED STATES, TOTAL[2]	3,204	348	10	9.2
South Atlantic	1,663	169	31	9.8
Delaware	2	1	5	2.8
Maryland	90	16	18	5.6
District of Columbia	4	1	18	2.5
Virginia[4]	473	55	33	8.6
North Carolina	289	28	27	10.2

48

South Carolina	385	26	48	15.0
Georgia	382	38	42	9.9
Florida	39	4	39	11.2
East South Central	1,103	125	32	8.8
Kentucky	211	38	29	5.5
Tennessee	239	34	26	7.1
Alabama	343	29	40	11.7
Mississippi	310	23	44	13.4

— Represents or rounds to zero.
NA Not available. Data on the number of all families are not available for
  Delaware, Virginia, Georgia, Kentucky, the Southwest territories, and for
  Allegheny, Calvert, and Somerset Counties in Maryland.
[1] Includes a small number of free black slaveholding families.
[2] Includes states and territories, not shown separately.
[3] Estimate.
[4] Includes area which is now West Virginia.

Source: U.S. Department of Commerce, Bureau of the Census (1979), p. 12.

an easily identified population typically creates patterns of oppression. In the economic sphere, this oppression involved the continuance of slavery and legitimating beliefs. Beliefs are most likely to be held fervently by those most immediately threatened by a change in the structural conditions that such beliefs legitimate. While large landowners would certainly be threatened, the smaller landowners and non-farm workers would be even more threatened by the sudden penetration of the labor market by free blacks. The result was that racist beliefs, as outlined in the last chapter, were maintained by virtually all southerners, even as these beliefs were challenged in the North.

The ideological attacks of northern abolitionists on the use of slaves in the southern economy were countered by a further codification in the South of antebellum beliefs emphasizing the "Sambo" stereotype of biologically inferior blacks only too willing to do the economic bidding of their white owners. Even inside the small intellectual circle of radical abolitionists, northern beliefs acknowledged the intellectual inferiority of blacks while opposing the proslavery doctrine. These differences in the northern and southern belief systems no doubt reflected the respective economic dependency of the northern and southern economies on slave labor. There were few blacks in the North, with the result that the economies of northern states would remain unaffected by abolition or the colonization of the black population, whereas the loss of slave labor would cause widespread disruption of the southern economy and lifestyle. Ideological codification of the "positive good" theory of slavery legitimated southern economic arrangements and fostered intense resistance to any change in these arrangements. In the North, blacks were believed to be inferior, but the abolition of slavery was seen as necessary, particularly since it posed no threat to the economic order. Only later in the twentieth century, when large numbers of blacks began to penetrate the northern job market, did racist beliefs come to dominate and to legitimate oppressive acts by northern whites.

The Civil War and Reconstruction

Only a war between the states was to penetrate the culturally legitimated economic system of the South. During the brief period of "Radical Reconstruction" after the Civil War, a considerable amount of forced equality was implemented by Congress; for the first time in their history in America, large numbers of blacks gained access to many skilled trades and began to assume ownership of farms. By 1890 there were almost 600,000 black farm operators in the United States and well over 130,000 black farm owners (Greene and Woodson, 1930:212–13). Even though legislative tides turned against blacks as early as 1877 and industrial jobs in the North convinced many of them to desert their newly acquired farms, blacks actually increased their numbers among farm operators and owners through 1920. By 1920 there were over 900,000 black farm operators in the United States and 218,612 black farm owners (Greene and Woodson, 1930:212–13).

As early as 1877, the U.S. Congress had altered its Reconstruction policies. As a result, progress towards economic emancipation was halted, then reversed (see chapter 4 for the details of this shift). For thirty years thereafter, though some operated and owned the poorest farms, blacks in the South experienced a worsening of their general economic situation. That black farmers actually controlled almost a million fewer acres in 1925 than in 1910 reflects this trend. During this same period, the numbers of blacks working as waiters, servants, laundresses, janitors, bootblacks, and in other menial jobs also declined (Greene and Woodson, 1930: 215–46). Blacks were systematically excluded from skilled non-farm occupations and were thrust into tenant farming or low-wage labor for white landowners or into menial labor and domestic work in both rural and urban areas.

Such a dramatic reversal of the economic policies of Radical Reconstruction was legitimized by a limited conception of "equality" and by the then dominant laissez-faire ideology which, along with the Social Darwinism of the late nineteenth century, allowed white economic interests to assert that blacks had been given "equal opportunity" and had demonstrated an inability to take advantage of these opportunities or to compete effectively against whites. Thus, further legislative and social intervention into the economic affairs of the South would impede the "natural biological struggle" as the races sought their respective ecological (economic) niches. Blacks were once again relegated to the most inferior economic positions because of their presumed intellectual inferiority.

Early Twentieth-Century Economic Oppression

At the turn of the twentieth century, 90 percent of all blacks still resided in the South, with 75 percent living under oppressive conditions in rural areas. For a number of reasons, the plight of blacks, especially those in rural areas, worsened dramatically during the early years of this century (Hamilton, 1964). The high birth rates of poor families began to exceed their ability to secure sufficient income in the depressed economy of the rural South. The nature of agriculture changed dramatically with mechanization and resulted in the displacement of much black labor. In the 1920s the cotton industry, on which many blacks depended for survival, was devastated by the boll weevil and began to move to the Southwest. These problems, coupled with discrimination in all other institutional spheres and increased acts of white violence against blacks, comprise the most important "push" factors that disposed blacks to migrate out of the South and into the urban areas of the North. By 1920 these "push factors" were combined with "pull factors" from northern cities, and the mass transformation of poor rural blacks into urban industrial workers was initiated.

Changes in the character of the American black work force began to appear between 1910 and 1920, when the proportion of blacks in agricultural as well as personal and domestic service jobs dropped. At the same time, the proportion of black workers in manufacturing, trade, and transportation industries increased. Through this period agriculture still remained the main employer of black labor. In 1920, 45 percent of blacks were employed in agriculture, with 22 percent in domestic service, another 20 percent in manufacturing, 11 percent in trade and transportation, and the remaining 2 percent in professional service (Greene and Woodson, 1930).

This shift in the distribution of black workers occurred primarily in response to economic forces in the North. During

World War I, European migration was curtailed, creating a labor shortage at the height of wartime production. Consequently, blacks came north in search of job opportunities in wartime industries. Another significant force was the use of blacks as strikebreakers to control the spread of the union movement. The combined operation of these forces encouraged the movement of blacks from the South to the North; yet such forces did not enable blacks to escape from the bottom ranks of the stratification system.

Wartime Production and Black Workers

The increase in economic opportunities during World War I created jobs for blacks, but such jobs were the most menial and low paying. Once wartime production ceased, blacks were the most likely to be laid off. Even during wartime production, blacks received lower wages than whites for comparable work as separate pay scales for blacks and whites were common. Blacks were also systematically kept from assuming supervisory or managerial positions. The North thus adopted the same employment strategies that had been used in the South since Reconstruction: (1) confinement of blacks to a limited range of occupations and (2) less pay for comparable work.

Such tactics were not necessarily desired by large-scale employers who, in all likelihood, would have been willing to employ blacks at a low wage, thereby forcing white wages to decline and owner profits to increase. But pressures from white workers were intense in both the economic and political arenas. The conflict between industrialists and white workers was most evident in the way blacks were used to inhibit the growth of the union movement.

The Union Movement and Black Workers

Blacks were either systematically excluded from the early phases of the union movement or relegated to all-black auxiliary unions. For example, Herbert Northrup (1944:3–5) developed this profile of union discrimination at the end of the 1930s:

> I. Union which excludes Negroes by provision in ritual: Machinists, International Association of (AFL)

II. Unions which exclude Negroes by provision in constitution:

    A. AFL affiliates

        Railroad Telegraphers, Order of

        Railway Mail Association

        Switchmen's Union of North America

        Wire Weavers' Protective Association, American

    B. Unaffiliated Organizations

        Locomotive Engineers, Brotherhood of

        Locomotive Firemen and Enginemen, Brotherhood of

        Railroad Trainmen, Brotherhood of

        Railroad Yardmasters of America

        Railroad Yardmasters of North America

        Railway Conductors, Order of

        Train Dispatchers' Association, American

III. Unions which habitually exclude Negroes by tacit consent:

    A. AFL affiliates

        Asbestos Workers, Heat and Frost Insulators

        Electrical Workers, International Brotherhood of

        Flint Glass Workers' Union, American

        Granite Cutters' International Association

        Plumbers and Steamfitters, United Association of Journeymen

    B. Unaffiliated Organizations

        Marine Firemen, Oilers, Watertenders, and Wipers' Association, Pacific Coast

        Railroad Shop Crafts, Brotherhood of

IV. Unions that afford Negroes only segregated auxiliary status:

    A. AFL Affiliates

        Blacksmiths, Drop Forgers and Helpers, Brotherhood of

        Boilermakers, Iron Shipbuilders, Welders, and Helpers, Brotherhood of

        Maintenance of Way Employees, Brotherhood of

        Railway Carmen of America, Brotherhood of

        Railway and Steamship Clerks, Freight Handlers, Express and Station Employees, Brotherhood of

        Rural Letter Carriers, Federation of

        Seafarers International Union

        Sheet Metal Workers' International Association

B. Unaffiliated Organizations
   Railroad Workers, American Federation of
   Rural Letter Carriers' Association

Such exclusion reflected not just "racist beliefs," as outlined in the last chapter. It also was the result of a perceived threat (whether real or imagined) that blacks would be willing to work for less, thus mitigating union demands. Industrialists and other employers escalated these fears by using blacks as strikebreakers (Bonacich, 1976).

Blacks were thus placed in an untenable position. They needed income and job experience; they could not join unions on an equal basis with whites; and they were forced to work as strikebreakers, thereby escalating white hostility toward them. The fact that some of the bloodiest "race riots" of American history occurred in the early decades of this century in the aftermath of strikebreaking activities attests to the hostility of whites towards blacks. Indeed, in 1919 alone, there were over twenty-five violent black-white confrontations in the North. Many of these were initiated by whites attacking blacks after a period of tension associated with strikes.

The Overall Pattern

In sum, the pattern of economic oppression is explained by the "push factors" associated with problems in southern agriculture and the "pull factors" associated with northern work opportunities in wartime production and strikebreaking. These forces help explain the pattern of black economic participation.

1. Black migration from the South to the North escalated in the first three decades of this century in response to economic opportunities.
2. Black participation in nonagricultural economic roles increased dramatically.
3. Black unemployment was less than white unemployment (Bonacich, 1976:35) since blacks could perform

menial jobs not occupied by whites and could be used as strikebreakers.[3]

4. Black wages were considerably lower than white wages.

This pattern did little to improve the economic plight of blacks, but it did much to arouse the antagonism of white labor against blacks. It is not surprising, therefore, that beliefs about blacks in the early decades of this century were extremely negative. But, there were some transformations in the situation of blacks that, in the long run, would operate to improve, if only minimally, the absolute level of deprivation of black workers. First, blacks became more than a "southern problem" as they migrated to other regions. Eventually, blacks' geographical dispersion would allow them to establish a broader geopolitical base. Second, the urbanization of blacks, even if in dilapidated tenement housing, would increase their influence within city governments. Third, blacks became increasingly nonagrarian, a fact that would eventually allow penetration into some unions. Yet, despite some absolute gains in economic conditions, the relative plight of blacks was not to decrease dramatically in later decades of the twentieth century.

Recent Forms of Economic Oppression

The post-World War II period has seen numerous apparent improvements in the economic situation of blacks, as many unions have opened their ranks to blacks, as civil rights legislation has proliferated, and as the number of college-educated blacks in the job market has increased. Yet, much of this change is illusory and does not reveal the true proportions of economic racism in contemporary America. For example, blacks are still overrepresented in farm and service occupations and underrepresented in professional and managerial occupations. Black unemployment is now typically twice that of whites (recall that it was one-half that of whites in earlier decades). Black pay scales are still lower than whites; college-educated blacks, on the average, still earn only a little more than high-school educated whites; and black income as a percentage of white income has actually declined. That the gap between white and black income is not narrowing as a result of the War on Poverty and other federal programs in the 1960s is illustrated in figure 3.1. While the average income of both blacks and whites has increased in the last few decades, blacks have lost ground to whites in terms of their relative earning power.

It can be argued, of course, that this kind of analysis is too general and that by treating blacks and whites as two amorphous groups, the economic gains made in the 1960s by "targeted" black groups are overshadowed. This may be the case, but income figures for black and white families in 1974 and 1977 suggest otherwise. The income gap between blacks and whites actually widened during this period, with black families earning 57 percent of white income in 1977 as compared to 60 percent in 1974. While undoubtedly there is a lag between institutional change and its impact on income and employment figures, the disadvantaged position of black workers in contemporary America cannot be explained as simply a lag phenomenon. On the contrary, economic discrimination remains built into the structure and culture of America's major economic institutions.

To appreciate economic discrimination in contemporary America, it is appropriate to ask: What avenues or channels to equal participation in the economy are available? And are any, or all, of these channels discriminatory? An examination of the three most general economic channels—opportunities for running a business, opportunities for securing jobs and promotions in the open job market, and opportunities within union job markets to find work and be promoted—reveal that even in the face of clear civil rights laws, much discrimination can be found. Because of the lag effects of changes in institutions, this present discrimination will continue to maintain the disadvantaged position of blacks for some time.

Business Opportunities

For many white Americans, owning and running a business has been one path to affluence. For blacks, however, this path to success is hazardous. And even when blacks do own busi-

Figure 3.1.
Median income of families, 1947 to 1980.

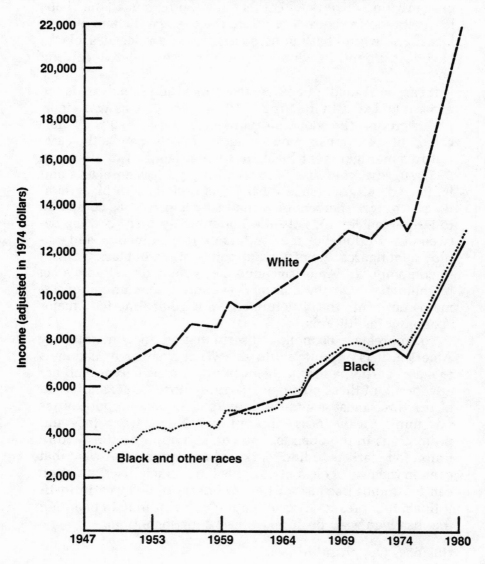

Source: U.S. Department of Commerce, Bureau of the Census (1979), p. 22; and U.S. Department of Commerce, Bureau of the Census (1982), pp. 49–50.

nesses, they tend to be labor-intensive proprietorships that are economically marginal. In 1972 there were an estimated 195,000 black-owned businesses in America, a figure that would be much higher if blacks owned businesses in proportion to their numbers. For example, the proportion of black-owned businesses to total businesses (excluding corporations) at that time was less than 3 percent (U.S. Department of Commerce, Bureau of the Census, 1979a:63; Brimmer, 1966).

It is more difficult for blacks than whites to secure credit, since the criteria used by lending agencies favor those with "white credentials" such as education, current collateral, and high credit ratings. While all small businesses are high-risk ventures, there is no evidence that black businesses in ghetto neighborhoods are any more risky than white ventures in white neighborhoods. For example, in 1964 the Small Business Administration began extending loans in terms of criteria other than credit history and collateral. Ninety-eight of 219 loans issued that year went to blacks. Surprisingly, only 8 of the 219 loans became delinquent, and none were liquidated—underscoring the unreliability and subtle racism built into current credit practices in white lending institutions (Foley, 1966; Holsendolph, 1979:19; Knowles and Prewitt, 1969:17).

More recently, blacks have had a tougher time securing business loans. For example, in 1973 there were 8,842 Small Business Administration loans made to minority business people, totaling almost $303 million. These are loans made by banking insitutions but guaranteed by the federal government. In 1977, however, there were only 6,072 such loans made to minority business people, though inflation bloated their total dollar amount to over $333 million. This is seen by many in the banking industry as a signal that bankers are increasingly reluctant to extend normal loans to black business people, even when the government offers to guarantee such loans (Holsendolph, 1979:29). Such economic policies keep existing black businesses small and make it extremely difficult for new businesses to stay afloat.

Opportunities for Securing Jobs

The barriers to black participation in the business sector have far-reaching consequences for the plight of blacks in other

sectors of the economy. One of the most important consequences is that black Americans become highly dependent
upon employment in white-dominated organizations where,
as the historical record shows, they have been subject to intense discrimination. Such discrimination is reflected in the
fact that since 1954 the black unemployment rate has consistently exceeded the 6 percent level which, according to
conventional economic "wisdom," signals serious difficulties
for the white work force. To illustrate the magnitude and con-
stancy of this problem, we have summarized the official government unemployment rates for black and white Americans
for selected years from 1948 to 1980.

Figure 3.2 shows that, regardless of the year, unemployment
rates in post-World War II years for blacks are about twice as
high as for whites, and that the gap between black and white
unemployment rates appears to be widening. Between 1977
and 1978, the total number of unemployed whites dropped
from 5.5 to 4.7 million. For blacks, there was no decline in
the 1.5 million persons out of work. During this period, the
official unemployment rate for blacks ranged from 12 to 13
percent; for whites, from 5 to 6 percent. In 1978 the official
black jobless rate was 2.3 times higher than the rate for whites,
the widest gap ever recorded (Hill, 1979:26). And in 1982,
early figures on the respective employment rates of blacks and
whites indicate an even larger gap (U.S. Department of Labor,
1982). The unofficial jobless count for blacks, which includes
discouraged workers—persons eligible to work but who are no
longer looking for work—is even higher. Including discouraged workers, 23 to 25 percent of all blacks are out of work.
This involves in excess of 3 million persons (Hill, 1979:27)
and signals a serious economic depression in the black community.

As alarming as the unemployment figures for adult blacks
are, the unemployment picture for young blacks is even worse.
The annual unemployment rate for black teenagers in 1978
was set at 37 percent and it has not gone down for several
years. The hidden joblessness rate for black teenagers in 1978
was estimated at 57 percent. These unemployment figures are
due in part to the rapid growth in the size of this black age

group in recent years, and in part to economic racism. The unemployment rate for white teenagers was also high in 1978 at 14 percent. But in recent years the joblessness rate for white youth has been decreasing (Hill, 1979:29). Bernard Anderson, in testimony before the House Subcommittee on Employment Opportunities, explained higher unemployment rates for black youth by pointing to "their disadvantages in educational attainment, geographic locations, and social service support. Discrimination, however, plays a major role in limiting the employment of black youth in better jobs" (Anderson, 1977:18).

Equally important is the underemployment of blacks who are able to find jobs. For example, in 1966, the latest year for which these estimates are available, the Kerner Commission reported that an additional $4.8 billion in income would be produced for blacks if their employment were upgraded to a level proportionate to whites with similar skills and credentials (Knowles and Prewitt, 1969:20). It is reasonable to assume this figure is presently much higher.

The Open Job Market

A number of structural forces have operated to oppress black Americans in the open job market. First, unskilled rural blacks migrated to the cities at just the time in America's economic development when large pools of unskilled industrial labor were decreasingly necessary. In contrast to earlier European migrants who were able to work their way out of poverty in readily available unskilled jobs, blacks were unable, except during the height of wartime production and strikebreaking efforts, to secure jobs. Second, just as blacks migrated to the deteriorating cores of America's cities (where they were forced to live because of housing discrimination), the economic and demographic trend in America was in the direction of suburbanization. Thus, industry and commerce began to move out of the city, drawing with it the white population, at the very time that blacks were moving into the cities in search of new economic opportunities. Because of housing discrimination in the suburbs, blacks could not move with whites to the emerging suburban industries; and because mass transit systems be-

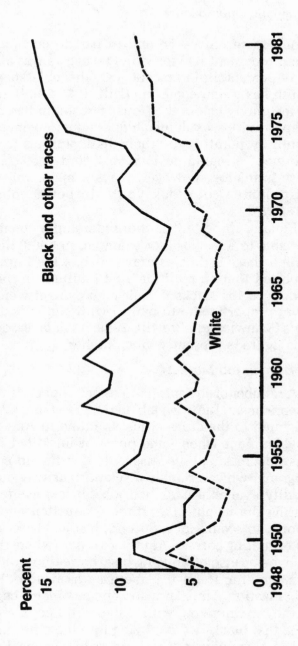

Figure 3.2.
Unemployment rates: 1948 to 1980 (annual averages).

Figure 3.2 (continued)

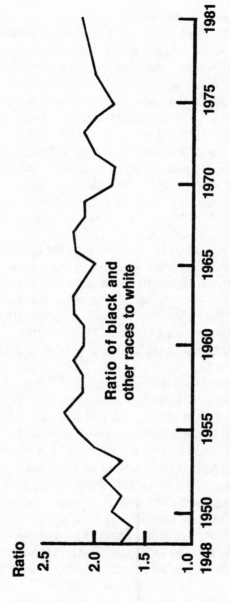

Ratio of black and other races to white

Source: U.S. Department of Commerce, Bureau of the Census (1979), p. 59; and U.S. Department of Labor, Bureau of Labor Statistics (1982), p. 58.

gan to deteriorate with America's growing dependency on the automobile, blacks could not easily commute to suburban jobs. Third, black Americans became an industrial labor pool after trade and industrial unions had become organized and had begun to exclude both white and black members.

Dominant beliefs of the late nineteenth century, rather than calling attention to the social and economic reasons for blacks' inability to become integrated into the job market, emphasized the character flaws of blacks, who again "exposed" their inability to "take advantage of opportunities and compete successfully against whites." In turn, such beliefs could be used to systematically exclude blacks from full economic participation, since they had "had their chance" and were no longer worthy of equal consideration.

In the private job market, this racism involved outright rejection of black applications for jobs in both blue- and white-collar occupations. And the discriminatory practices of private business have been compounded by the policies of state and private employment agencies where, as a number of studies have revealed, blacks are not given occupational classifications commensurate with their skills, are likely to receive fewer job referrals than whites, and are less likely than equivalently educated whites to be referred to job openings in businesses.

Beyond such open racism is a subtle and yet profoundly important institutional racism in the job market: the biasing of criteria for what constitutes a good worker in favor of the cultural traits of whites. For example, since written tests for jobs are constructed by whites, they discriminate against those of a different cultural background. Or, to take another example, white speech styles and personal demeanor—which, in reality, are seldom related to actual job performance—are considered "appropriate" in certain jobs. Even the overuse of formal educational credentials—which, again, are often unnecessary for most routine jobs—discriminate against blacks and other groups that cannot afford higher education. Thus, there is an invidious racism built into the hiring practices of American economic organizations, a racism that perpetuates the disadvantaged position of black Americans.

The government sector of the economy has been almost as

discriminatory as the private job sector. One form of discrimination has been the failure of government to enforce civil rights codes even for organizations doing contract business with the government. More directly, while blacks are slightly overrepresented in government jobs, they are highly underrepresented in the better paying administrative positions.

The Union Job Market

Compounding this private and governmental racism in the open job market are the discriminatory practices in the job market controlled by labor unions. Because unions are the only avenue for entry into most skilled blue-collar jobs and many unskilled occupations, racial discrimination in this sector of the economy has profound consequences for the economic prospects of minority Americans, particularly blacks. The fact that of the over 11 million black workers, less than 20 percent are members of trade unions suggests the extent of union discrimination, especially when it is recognized that the vast majority of the black work force is blue-collar and thus desirous of union membership.[4]

While the general policies of national labor organizations such as the AFL-CIO are antidiscriminatory, these policies are frequently ignored by union locals. Craft and trade unions, which have the strongest local structure, are the most discriminatory, with few blacks involved in such trades as plumbers, carpenters, electricians, printers, metal workers, and machinists (Schaffler et al., 1970:44). The most prevalent strategy for discrimination against blacks is exclusion from apprenticeship programs. For example, the U.S. Commission on Civil Rights reported in the 1960s that of the 1,667 apprentices in the St. Louis craft unions, only 7 were black; in Baltimore, of the 750 building trade apprentices, 20 were black; and in both Atlanta and Baltimore, no blacks were in the apprenticeship programs of the iron workers, the plumbers, the Brotherhood of Electrical Workers, the sheet metal workers, and the painters union (Knowles and Prewitt, 1969:23).

Because industrial unions such as the United Automobile Workers organize workers on an industry-wide basis, and because much of the work performed involves no apprenticeship, many blacks have been able to join industrial unions and get jobs. However, the apprenticeship programs of these industrial unions—which lead to higher paying, skilled jobs—are often discriminatory. For example, in one Detroit auto manufacturing plant, 23 percent of the workers were black, but out of 289 apprenticeships, only 1 was held by a black worker (Knowles and Prewitt, 1969:23). Thus, even in "liberal" industrial unions where blacks are union members, they are more likely than whites to be kept at the lower paying positions.

The Economics of Oppression

We have examined economic discrimination at the outset for the simple reason that one's place in the economy determines access to valued resources, such as money, power, and prestige. The exclusion of blacks from skilled economic roles has prevented them from securing these valued resources. Moreover, without steady employment and an above subsistence income, it becomes difficult to better the options of offspring, thus perpetuating a cycle of oppression.

Once institutionalized, economic discrimination can only be eliminated through the exertion of political power. That is, through the powers of government—coercive, regulatory, and financial—sectors of the economy can be compelled to admit blacks. Unfortunately, political enfranchisement is dependent upon economic position. And since blacks have not possessed economic resources, they have had great difficulty in mobilizing the political system toward their interests. These difficulties are documented in the next chapter on political oppression.

Summary

Obstacles in business, open employment, and union sectors of the economy represent a massive form of institutional racism. Cut off from the normal channels of economic participation, blacks are often forced to take menial and seasonal work that offers only the minimal wage and few, if any, fringe benefits. Current beliefs in America support this situation. Although "liberal environmentalism" acknowledges the detrimental impact of discriminatory experiences on blacks' ability to enter the job market, "equal opportunity" beliefs, coupled with widespread "backlash" attitudes, allow employers, unions, and credit agencies to discriminate because blacks do not meet the criteria for economic participation. Equal opportunity has thus become a belief justifying "equal" and "even-handed" treatment of blacks and whites in terms of criteria that favor whites. While dominant beliefs have become less severe and blatant, they still operate in a subtle and profound way to legitimate institutional arrangements that impede the full participation of blacks in the economy.

CHAPTER FOUR

Political Oppression

Change in oppressive institutional arrangements comes through the exercise of political power. Yet, one of the ironies of oppression is that those who could most benefit by change seldom possess enough power to bring it about. Despite the large size of the black population in the United States, its capacity to generate political influence has been limited. The reasons for this relative powerlessness are to be found in historical processes that have created a political system that is unresponsive to the plight of the poor in general and to the black in particular. As a result, the elimination of oppression in other institutional structures has not been possible.

Political Oppression and Black Protest

Political oppression involves efforts by dominant groups to deny the access of minority populations to power. The nature and degree of oppressive arrangements are understood best by examining the range of responses by the oppressed, for power is often illusive until it is mobilized to either generate or resist change.

The general forms of black protest have revolved around two types of political efforts (Cox, 1950; Hinds, 1971), one designed to integrate blacks into the mainstream of American society, the other designed to radically alter institutional arrangements and black patterns of organization. The sporadic and varying degree of success and failure in these forms of political resistance highlight, as we will come to see, the nature of political oppression of blacks.

The Integrationist Approach

Integrationists advocate working for change and "making the best of it" within the existing political system. To date, this has been the pole around which most black Americans fix their political positions. Many of the great black leaders have been integrationists who protested racial oppression and worked toward political change, but did so without advocating dramatic alteration of the political system. Frederick Douglass, W. E. B. Dubois, A. Phillip Randolph, and Martin Luther King, Jr. are the most visible representatives of thousands of such black Americans who could be called "protest integrationists."

Other integrationists are more conservative and advocate working for change not so much through protest as through tolerance of white racism. The house slaves, slave artisans, and black plantation preachers were early "conservative integrationists." They had ascended to power within the racist traditions of the Old South and they felt that the best way to make additional gains was by using their limited resources to quietly help themselves and others within the system. But their power was derived directly from the white plantation owners and managers and from the institution of slavery itself. This connection made the process of change slow and costly. Booker T. Washington was the most powerful of all the conservative integrationists. In the first part of the twentieth century, he rose to a position of national prominence by advocating that blacks genially overlook racist aspects of white culture and work hand-in-hand with whites for their mutual benefit.

Radical Approaches

The earliest advocates of radical change were the slaves who resisted their captors during the boat passage to America or after arriving in America. Right up to the Civil War, slaves continued to run away from southern plantations, many through the Underground Railroad run by northern Quakers and black radicals like Harriet Tubman. Tubman, a powerful woman possessing considerable strength and military skill, personally led several groups of runaway slaves from the South to the North via the Railroad.

Slave Revolts. Slave revolts were common in the United States throughout the eighteenth and nineteenth centuries. Usually a handful of male slaves would be involved in isolated incidents where they were provoked and rose up in arms to escape or to protect themselves from unbearable tyranny. The Denmark Vesey conspiracy of 1822 and the Nat Turner insurrection of 1831 are notable examples of this type of radical action. In the swamps of the South, especially in Florida, runaway slaves were known to aggregate and to form their own communities or merge with Native American communities (Degler, 1971).

All types of early radical black protest were violently opposed and largely controlled by white America. Runaway slaves were diligently pursued by their white owners and, when retrieved, were severely punished and sometimes sold into an even more demeaning form of slavery. The control of runaway slaves was supported by national law, which required all U.S. citizens to aid in identifying and apprehending runaways. In fact, returned runaway slaves were often treated with hostility by fellow slaves on the plantation for bringing closer scrutiny and tighter control down upon those who chose to remain docile. The leaders of early slave revolts were in almost all cases rounded up by white vigilante groups (forerunners of the modern-day KKK and southern nightriders) and tortured or killed. The slave communities in southern swamps and in Florida were broken up by military action. The best known of these massacres of slaves was the Battle of Negro Fort in western Florida in 1816, when over one thousand runaway slaves were attacked by the Fourth U.S. Infantry and their Indian allies. During the siege of the community and after its surrender, nearly all the blacks were killed (Foster, 1959:100-101).

The Back-to-Africa Movement. In the early 1900s another radical group was formed by black Jamaican immigrant Marcus Garvey. It was Garvey's position that blacks could never be treated fairly in a country where they were in the minority. He advocated a "back-to-Africa" movement that would reclaim lands in Africa for American blacks who would set up their own government and other social institutions. For a few years Garvey attracted a large following in the United States, but his business ventures were apparently filled with corruption. In 1922 he was indicted in a federal court for illegal use of the U.S. mails. He was found guilty and sentenced to five years in prison. He spent two years of his sentence in an Atlanta prison and then was pardoned by President Calvin Coolidge and deported to Jamaica. With the demise of Garvey, his back-to-Africa movement lost momentum and vanished.

The Black Muslims. In the mid-1930s, another radical change movement emerged among the Black Muslims. From the outset, Muslims advocated separatism from the "white devil" and avoided racial integration. Under the leadership of Elijah Muhammed, the Muslims went about building a separate black nation in America. They currently sponsor and encourage all-black or black-dominated business ventures in real estate, entertainment, the food industry, and other areas of commerce. By the mid-1960s, Muslims were estimated by one source to have almost 100,000 members (Franklin, 1974:474). Today, there are no accurate estimates of the size of Muslim membership, although many place it at well over a million.

Other Radical Groups. In 1966 another radical change group, the Black Panther party, was formed in Oakland, California. The party adopted a revolutionary Marxist-Leninist ideology and encouraged black people to arm themselves and throw over the capitalist leadership of the United States. Other radical change groups that formed in the 60s included the Republic of New Africa group, the Revolutionary Action Movement, and the Los Angeles-based U.S. Organization, which advocated cultural rather than military liberation from white society (Pinkney, 1971:247–52).

To date, however, membership in radical groups has been small in comparison with integrationist groups. This disparity can be attributed at least in part to the high attrition rate among radical black leaders who have become the targets of vigorous efforts at prosecution and persecution by local and national government. For example, many of the more militant leaders like Garvey, Eldridge Cleaver, Bobby Seale, and others ran afoul of the law and were silenced. Others, like Fred Hampton, were killed in shoot-outs with urban police forces. The government, too, has curtailed membership in radical groups by taking small steps to improve the lot of black Americans.

Summary

Radical efforts to change oppressive arrangements have been effectively resisted by dominant whites—ample testimony to their relative power. In contrast, integrationist efforts, which are more conservative, have met resistance but have resulted in some gains for black Americans. The history of political oppression is thus marked by the failure of radical resistance and by the sporadic and partial success of integrationist efforts to change political arrangements.

Early Forms of Political Oppression

Before their capture and exportation to the New World as slaves, black Africans had a long political history and well-developed political empires. Efforts to invade these political systems in search of slaves date back to 5000 B.C. with the activities of Egyptians and Persians in North Africa. The modern period of enslavement began in the late fourteenth century with the Spanish and Portuguese.

At first, the slavers tried on their own to capture blacks from the villages of the western coastal region of Africa. But this practice was costly, and it provided a source of considerable ill will towards slavers upon their return for more slaves. A more expedient and efficient alternative was befriending coastal political leaders, who would assist slavers in exchange for goods and commodities. These leaders sold into permanent bondage their own undesirables and those whom they captured from inland villages and perhaps from their political enemies. In the sixteenth century, the number of slaves secured in this way and imported from Africa to the New World appears to have been around 900,000. In the seventeenth century, approximately 2.75 million African slaves were imported. In the eighteenth century, at the height of the African slave trade, as many as 7 million natives were captured. In the nineteenth century, another 3.25 million Africans were taken as slaves (Franklin, 1974:44).

As an aside to the emergence of slavery in America, we should note that the slave trade devastated the political development of many African states. Tribes, petty states, and kingdoms were simply overrun in the accelerated slave hunts of the eighteenth century. Moreover, the slave trade gave European nations a real incentive for investigating, invading, and then colonizing Africa, with the result that Africa's political development was further arrested and distorted in ways that still pose profound problems of political unity and integration. Thus, by the end of the slave trade, the political institutions of each slave's homeland were either disrupted or corrupted.

The Institutionalization of Slavery in America

The first African slaves were brought to Virginia in the mid-seventeenth century. Before 1661, Africans were not true slaves because, as Franklin (1974:56) notes, blacks were listed in the early census counts as indentured servants for whom manumission after a period of servitude was common. By 1661 and 1662, however, the Virginia Assembly passed legislation that made African blacks slaves for life and dictated that children born to them in the New World would also be enslaved. Similar legislation was enacted in Massachusetts in 1641, Connecticut in 1650, Rhode Island in 1652, New York in 1665, South Carolina in 1682, New Hampshire in 1714, North Carolina in 1715, Delaware in 1721, and Georgia in 1749 (Foster, 1954:37).

In each of these states, as well as in the others that later embraced slavery, a corresponding set of "slave codes" was enacted by state legislatures. These codes denied slaves the right to own property, to marry, to seek relief in court, to seek free passage, and to bear arms to protect themselves. It was under these conditions of political oppression that most black Americans lived until the Civil War.

But even before the Civil War, many slaves gained freedom—some by earning money with which to pay off their masters, others by running away to the North or to South America, and still others by fighting for the young nation in its war of independence with England. It was these early freed men and women who formed the first nucleus of black political dissent from which all American black political action has since flowed.

Political Oppression During the Revolutionary War

Before the revolutionary war, it appeared that the American colonies were taking a decisive step against slavery when the Continental Congress outlawed the importation of foreign slaves beginning in 1776. This action encouraged many blacks, free and slave alike, to support the young American nation in its first war against England. When fighting broke out in 1775, blacks were involved in all early military actions and could be seen fighting side-by-side with whites. Later in the year, however, General Washington and his advisors issued an order that all blacks were to be relieved of military duty, and under strong protest from blacks and some whites, black soldiers were sent home.

The British took advantage of this situation. Through their agents in South Carolina, Virginia, and Maryland, they offered freedom to any slave who would cross over the lines and take up arms against the colonies. This move by the British precipitated a massive flow of slaves to the other side that did not stop until 1781, when the British were driven into the sea. When it became clear that slaves were fleeing in wholesale lots to the English side, Washington and his generals softened their policies by allowing the reenlistment of some former black soldiers.

Later in the war, as white soldiers came into short supply, some experienced freedmen and a few slaves were allowed to enlist. In the North, blacks were often offered manumission for fighting the English. In the North and South alike, slaves were eventually allowed to go to war in place of their masters. And, in many cases, slaves were bought at inflated prices from their masters by the federal government to be used as soldiers. Through these means and through voluntary enlistments by patriotic blacks, about 5,000 blacks, out of a total of 300,000 American soldiers, fought in the revolutionary war.

Most enlisted blacks were integrated into white units and allowed to fight and otherwise serve beside whites. A few all-black companies were formed, but they were rare. Where all-black units did exist, their officers were always white—a tradition that was not broken until World War II.

Following the revolutionary war, some slaves who had fought on the side of the Americans realized significant gains. The greatest gains were by those slaves who took advantage of the breach in political control brought about by the fighting and fled to the North, to England and its possessions, or to South America. There are no accurate records on the number of slaves who fled, but in some states as many as one half of the slaves who were in residence before the fighting, escaped.

Many slave soldiers who had fought for the American cause were freed by their masters after the British were defeated, but especially in the South, returning soldiers were sometimes enslaved again by deceitful owners and managers. Yet, in some states, black soldiers received better treatment. This was the case in Virginia, where a law freeing all slaves who had fought on the American side during the war was passed in 1783. In other northern states, manumission and antislavery societies grew. For a very brief period, a wave of antislavery sentiment swept across North America.

The promise of abolishing slavery that had been implied by the Continental Congress in 1775 when it banned imported slaves was not realized by the Constitutional Convention of 1787. In fact, several of the articles of the Constitution that emerged from the convention acknowledged slavery and even went so far as to insure the return of runaway slaves to their owners. Thus, the War of Independence secured the freedom only of white Americans and a handful of black soldiers. The agreements made at the Constitutional Convention paved the way for the strengthened federal Fugitive Slave Law of 1793, which provided for the punishment of runaway slaves and required all citizens to participate in their return. In the years that followed, as the federal Constitution was amended to guarantee basic rights to working-class Americans, antislavery sentiment was ignored. At the end of the first great American war, blacks were still largely left in bondage, and even the few who had secured their "freedom" were not allowed to vote or to otherwise participate in American political life.

Growth of the Cotton Industry and the Rise of Southern Slavery

After the revolutionary war, the institution of slavery slowly died out in the northern United States. The North was developing an industrial system based upon factories and high technology for which slaves were not considered a suitable work force.

In 1793, a northern school teacher, Eli Whitney, invented the cotton gin and revolutionized both the southern cotton industry and the structure of slavery. The cotton gin could clean up to a thousand times as much cotton per day as could a slave working by the traditional hand method, thereby eliminating a chronic bottleneck in the production of cotton. The cotton gin also allowed for the rapid expansion of large cotton plantations into areas previously held by small southern farmers and into the new lands opening up in the West.

These changes in the southern cotton industry, coupled with the 1775 ban on imported slaves, had two important effects on slavery in the South. First, Whitney's cotton gin stimulated a short period of rapid growth in the southern cotton industry. In so doing, it enabled the South to retain its tenuous control over American commerce and federal politics for an additional half century. Indeed, the southern politicians and landowning industrialists used this advantage to nullify, until 1861, the growing abolitionist movement in the North. Second, the ban on imported slaves, rather than putting a halt to slavery, increased the price of the average slave from $300 in 1800 to around $1,500 by 1860. This made it much more difficult for slaves to buy their freedom and, in general, lessened the national rate of manumission. The new prices in the slave market made owning slave vessels and underwriting expeditions to Africa a highly attractive, if illegal, business. These conditions guaranteed a large number of merchants a high profit, assuring a steady flow of African slaves into the southern United States long after the ban of 1775.

This struggle between the factory based, high technology industrialists of the North and their allies, the abolitionists, on the one side, and the rejuvenated southern cotton industry, on the other, grew worse and finally resulted in the Civil War. But the period between 1820 and 1861 was marked by compromise efforts between the North and the South to resolve the slave issue more peaceably. For example, in the Missouri Compromise of 1820, Maine was admitted to the union as a free state while Missouri was opened as a new slave territory. The enacting legislation included a clause specifying that escaped slaves should be returned to their owners rather than allowed to remain on free soil.

Another effort to resolve the problem of coexisting free and enslaved blacks was the formation in 1816 of the American Society for the Colonization of the Free People of Color of the United States. The purpose of this southern-dominated organization was to encourage free blacks to return to Africa. In the North, free blacks were tolerated, but their presence in America was not looked upon as a desirable situation by most white citizens. In the South, powerful slave owners believed that the large number of veteran free blacks had to be eliminated, lest they spur insurrection among the slaves. The Colonization Movement, as it has come to be known, lasted from 1820 until around 1852. With funds allocated from Congress, an African state, Liberia, was established, and blacks were recruited and given free passage back to their "homeland." By 1833, fewer than three thousand blacks had been sent back to Africa through this program, and by 1852 the number had risen to only eight thousand (Foster 1954:92). However, the idea of deporting large numbers of blacks remained a popular one among northern and southern whites throughout the nineteenth century.

Early Black Movements

Except for the brief period of Radical Reconstruction following the Civil War, blacks were excluded from mainstream political life in the United States for the entirety of the nineteenth century. In the North, as slavery ceased, the vote was still retained for whites only. Moreover, free northern blacks weathered wholesale discrimination on the job, in school, at church, and in the political arena. In the South, until 1865, most blacks were enslaved. The few freedmen were treated harshly and watched closely, and mainstream political activity for them was out of the question.

Yet, in such northern cities as Chicago, Philadelphia, and Washington, D.C., and in some southern cities, such as New Orleans, Richmond, and Atlanta, a strong black middle class was growing, and it was looking for avenues of political expression. This early search culminated in the American Negro Convention Movement that began in 1817 and lasted until the Civil War. At first the movement was local, with groups of black delegates meeting in Richmond and Philadelphia. At these meetings they formulated political policy and discussed ways to take their views to the federal government. The movement came together to protest slavery, attempts at colonization, and discrimination against free blacks in the North. By 1833 the delegates were meeting annually in major northern cities and were attending from all over the country. At the conventions, delegates worked with antislavery groups to lobby for abolition; they created the first black national political organization, the American Society of Free Persons of Color; and they provided a forum for the first generation of national political figures to rise from their midst. Out of the movement came Harriet Tubman, a leader of the Underground Railroad; Samuel E. Cornish, publisher of the first black American newspaper; and

Frederick Douglass, a runaway slave who became a newspaper editor, minor government official, and the parent of the black protest movement.

Black Churches. Around 1775, all-black contingents of Methodists and Baptists began meeting together. In the South such meetings were watched closely by white overseers, for there was a tradition of using black ministers by plantation owners and managers to keep slaves in line. Ministers whose gospel favored cooperation with the slave system and who believed it best for slaves to expect a better lot in life "in the bye-and-bye" were favored by the white owners. Black ministers who were suspected of fomenting insurrection were tortured or killed.

The spirituality of black Americans could not be crushed and shaped into a safe tool of the slavers. Indeed, from their outset black churches were the seat of political activity. The First Baptist church in Montgomery, Alabama, is a good example. In slave days, the church was a station on the Underground Railroad and served as a meeting place for black political action groups in the Montgomery area. After the Civil War, the First Baptist housed Alabama's first integrated constitutional convention. And more recently, Ralph Abernathy, its minister in 1957, joined another Montgomery minister, Martin Luther King, Jr., to support Rosa Parks in her boycott of the city bus system. Other black churches all over the South repeated First Baptist's role in providing a political life for their members. In the North, all-black churches were active in antislavery, abolitionist, and other antiracist movements. Black northern church members led the way in building schools and pressing for political and civil rights.

Black Newspapers. Black newspapers were another new source of political action. In 1827, the first black newspaper, *Freedom's Journal,* was printed by Samuel E. Cornish and his partner, John B. Russwurm. The *Journal* found readers among urban, middle-class blacks and soon became a success. Other black papers and journals were published in most American cities with large concentrations of black workers. These papers waged a bitter fight against slavery and the colonization movement. Indeed, they provided a much-needed means of public expression for the black leaders of the time.

It was through these outlets of political expression that Frederick Douglass emerged as a political force. He had escaped from slavery in the South around 1838. Having been a house slave trained in speech and writing, he practiced his art by writing political tracts for the black newspapers of the late 1830s. Eventually, he opened his own newspaper, the *North Star*. In it, as well as in other newspapers, he spoke powerfully against slavery, racism, and the complicity of the federal government in perpetuating these evils. At the Negro Conventions and at every other available forum, Douglass decried the human waste of slavery and proposed programs for its abolition. He was, of course, not alone in these activities, for scores of intellectual and political leaders rose from the black masses during the nineteenth century. But none garnered public attention or pierced the defense of the federal government like Frederick Douglass. Except for him, black political and social leaders were ignored by the national government, and their impact upon national politics throughout this period was negligible. Indeed, if the widening split between the North and the South had not been based upon irreconcilable economic issues, it is likely that the abolitionist cause would have been ignored by the government for another hundred years.

To illustrate the unresponsiveness of the government to black leaders, Congress passed in 1850 an even harsher Fugitive Slave Act. Like the Slave Law of 1793 that it replaced, the new act required that runaway slaves, wherever found in the United States, be returned to their owners. But the new act also made it a crime for free citizens not to actively engage in the pursuit of runaways. To many citizens in the North, the Fugitive Slave Act of 1850 made it impossible for them to avoid the issue of slavery. Southern plantation owners, through their powerful representation in Congress, had in effect deputized every American citizen to pursue runaway slaves. This policy represented a considerable inconvenience for most whites who wanted to stay away from blacks altogether. And for the highly moral, such as the Quakers, it made the very act of living a

criminal violation. In later years, this law may have disposed
many white Northerners to fight in the war against the South.

The Civil War

The war was officially initiated by the South, ostensibly in
reaction to the election in 1860 of Abraham Lincoln as president of the United States. Lincoln was the candidate of the
newly formed Republican party and had beaten the proslavery
and southern-backed Democratic candidate, Stephen A. Douglas, in a close race. While Lincoln in the 1850s had occasion-
ally spoken out in public against slavery, it was widely known
that he was an appeasement candidate. He favored allowing
southern slavery to continue, and felt that the issue of slavery
was not sufficiently important to cause a war between the
North and the South. But before he took office, southerners
withdrew from Congress and high positions in the federal military. They formed the Confederate States and created their
own army. The South was preparing to exclude the North from
its economic and political affairs and to restore the Democratic
party to its place of national power. The South waited for a
brief time and then attacked Fort Sumter on April 12, 1861.
This battle started the Civil War of 1861–1865, which pitted
the military forces of the nation's two major regions in a succes-
sion of battles to determine national economic priorities and
the fate of slavery. Blacks, of course, were caught in the middle,
but they did what they could to fight for their freedom.

The Emancipation Proclamation came in September 1862,
long after hostilities had begun. Lincoln and his advisors decided to issue a statement freeing the southern slaves only
after it had become apparent that it would be extremely difficult, if not impossible, to win the war without doing so. At
the outset of the war there was little apparent intent on Lincoln's part to free the slaves. Indeed, he appears to have favored
financial compensation of slave owners and a large-scale program of African colonization for freed blacks.

In the early years of the war, it was both Union and Confederate government policy to exclude slaves from the military,
although blacks were used extensively by both sides as laborers, service personnel, servants, and spies. This policy finally

changed in 1863, when it became difficult in the North to draft sufficient numbers of white soldiers to meet the needs of the military. The New York draft riots of 1863 are typical of the social environment that precipitated the government's changing policy towards blacks. In New York before 1863, blacks were excluded from the draft, but at the same time, they were often employed by industrialists as strikebreakers. Under these conditions, working whites became highly reluctant to leave their homes and go to war, especially to fight for the emancipation of more blacks who could migrate to northern cities and be used by capitalists to cheapen the worth of white labor. This situation resulted in a series of riots that pitted striking white workers, who had been drafted into the army, against black workers who had come to replace them in their now vacant jobs. Variations of this scene were repeated in New Jersey, Chicago, Cleveland, Detroit, Buffalo, and Boston. As a result, changes in the law allowed blacks to be drafted into military service.

After the change in military policy, many blacks joined the U.S. Army or U.S. Navy. Even more black slaves were bought at discount prices by the federal government and conscripted into military service. It was not until 1864, however, that the U.S. government agreed to pay black soldiers at the same rate as white soldiers for service at similar ranks. As was the tradition by this time, blacks were segregated into fighting or labor units led by white officers. By the end of the Civil War, it is estimated that 186,000 blacks had enlisted in the Union Army. About 93,000 of those had been "recruited" from the Confederate States, 40,000 enlisted from border states, and 53,000 drawn to the war from the North (Franklin, 1974:230). While no such quantitative data are available for the South, a few blacks did serve among Confederate military forces. More typically, they served as cooks, laborers, messengers, and non-military workers for white troops. And in fact, many of the more affluent southern officers took an entourage of black slave servants with them as they moved about during the war.

Throughout the war, masses of blacks fled the South and crossed Union Army lines to seek protection. Many of the more able were conscripted into military service, while others were cloistered together and treated in discretionary ways by the officers in charge (since there was no government policy on this issue). Just behind the Union lines, northern philanthropic organizations provided aid for the refugees and offered formal instruction in religion and other ways of "civilized society." At first this work was done by fragmented groups, buttressed by donations and recruits from practically every northern religious organization. After the war, the administration of these services was combined into the American Freedmen's Aid Commission. Later this program was taken over by the U.S. government.

In 1865, Congress created the Freedmen's Bureau and allocated funds to provide aid for freed southern blacks. In rapid fashion, offices of the bureau were set up all over the South to aid blacks in reconstructing their lives and to assure their access to political power at state and local levels. Freedmen's Bureau offices in the South were largely staffed by northern Radical Republicans, who were not afraid to use the courts or the Union Army to correct social and political inequities.

The Reconstruction Period (1865–1900)

For about ten years after the war, conditions improved dramatically for American blacks under Radical Reconstruction. In the South—supported by Union troops occupying North Carolina, South Carolina, Georgia, Florida, Alabama, Mississippi, and Texas—workers for the Freedmen's Bureau set about registering black voters and encouraging educated and ambitious blacks to run for political office. In the North in 1865, the Thirteenth Amendment abolishing slavery was adopted. And, although a fierce battle over the shape of Reconstruction policy was developing between Lincoln and his successor, Andrew Johnson, on the one hand, and Congress, on the other, it was generally agreed that the most powerful southern plantation owners and their Confederate political allies should be disenfranchised, at least for awhile. But as early as 1865, when Lincoln was assassinated and Johnson became president, the seeds of the failure of Reconstruction were planted.

Positive Aspects. Much that occurred during this period,

however, was on the positive side. Blacks had wanted "forty acres and a mule," but much of the now vacant plantation land was bought up in large tracts by railroads and other northern industrial and banking interests. Instead, blacks got share-cropping arrangements on marginal farmland and the right to vote. Between 1866 and 1876, millions of southern blacks registered for the first time and exercised their right to vote. At the national level this was translated into blind support for white candidates of the Republican party. There were some black representatives elected to the U.S. Congress, but they were few in number and at no time totaled more than seven. In the North no blacks were elected to such high posts.

Between 1870 and 1881, two black men served the state of Mississippi in the U.S. Senate. Almost eight hundred blacks were elected to state offices in the South during Reconstruction. Most served for short terms in the lower houses, but a few rose to places of prominence and power. The records show that wherever blacks outnumbered whites, many were elected to local offices.

Another important source of support for the brief Radical Reconstruction effort came from the passage of the Civil Rights Act by Congress in March 1866. Among its most important provisions, the act extended full citizenship to all persons born in the U.S., except for Native Americans. The act also provided funds for carrying on Reconstruction programs in the South. President Johnson vetoed the act, but was overridden by Congress. In 1868 the act became the Fourteenth Amendment to the U.S. Constitution. The amendment has at most times been interpreted to award blacks the right to vote in state and federal elections.

Encouraged by these new laws, and spurred on by Frederick Douglass and other black Radical Reconstructionists, black political leaders developed new roots in their segregated churches and other political organizations. Perhaps the most important event in this respect was the birth of W. E. B. Dubois in 1868 in Massachusetts. It was Dubois who would rise to the top of black national politics at the turn of the century and lead the next stage of the fight against American racism.

Negative Aspects. Many forces and events worked against

the egalitarian reconstruction of the South. For example, as early as 1865 eight states, under the direction of President Johnson, adopted reconstruction plans that included "black codes" designed to deny blacks their basic civil rights. These codes were based on the earlier slave codes that had been used to keep blacks ignorant, without property, and physically vulnerable to violence. While these plans were blocked for awhile by Congress, they allowed antiblack forces in the South an early means of expression and political organization after their defeat in the war.

In 1865, disfranchised officers of the defeated Confederate Army formed the Ku Klux Klan in Pulaski, Tennessee. Although Congress, with some help from the federal courts, tried to bring the Klan under control, its popularity allowed it to spread across the white South. The Klan was a modern version of a slave-era enforcement technique. In the slave days, white workers often were incited by their employers to visit black dissidents and "suspects" in the night to beat, torture, and kill them in order to keep others in line. During the Reconstruction period, these vigilantes hid behind white veils to protect their secrecy. The Klan's violence became the prototype for other white-dominated southern action groups that were formed to resist Reconstruction.

In 1875, the tide turned heavily against the cause of freedom and justice for southern blacks. Early in the year, the Tennessee legislature adopted a pioneering piece of Jim Crow legislation that required blacks to be segregated from whites for all purposes of public instruction. It provided for segregated churches and forced blacks to sit in separate quarters while riding on all public conveyances. The law in its entirety extended in a negative way into every facet of social life. For awhile, Congress fought off state-level Jim Crow legislation by passing a civil rights law that outlawed racial discrimination in public places and on public transportation systems. As long as federal troops loyal to the North were positioned in the South, military and federal court decisions could be used to enforce this legislation. But public and nighttime violence increased against blacks, against their "carpetbagger" Freedmen's Bureau associates, and against "scalawag" southern whites who consorted with them. This kind of activity forced many blacks to refrain from voting in elections and to withdraw their candidacy for public office. With these acts the decline of Reconstruction began.

In 1877, President Rutherford B. Hayes agreed to withdraw federal troops who remained in the South and to lessen the role of the federal government in the affairs of the South. After this change of position by the federal government, racism and violence towards blacks increased throughout the country.

In the North, the contested issue was the use of blacks as nonunion strikebreakers. In the South, blacks were blamed for the humilities that had followed defeat in the war. In fact, in the minds of many northerners and southerners alike, blacks not only had failed to show the ability and inclination to become full citizens, but also were to blame for much of what troubled the nation.

One result was the initial exclusion of blacks from the union movement. For example, the American Federation of Labor, formed in 1881, soon became the dominant labor union in the land, primarily in the North. Drawing its membership from skilled workers and craftsmen who had the inside track for jobs and promotions in the factory system, the AFL feared competition from skilled black immigrants. Consequently, the AFL formally barred blacks from membership and discouraged their independent organization of unions. Blacks did experience some success in joining smaller unions of less skilled workmen, but as the AFL grew in prominence and national power, many of these early gains were lost. This trend left blacks in the North with the options of working around the fringes of industry at the lowest paying and most dangerous jobs, working as strikebreakers, or not working (see previous chapter for details).

In the South, more direct acts by government were taken to disfranchise blacks. For example, in its 1890 constitutional convention, Mississippi followed Tennessee's lead in developing Jim Crow legislation by adopting a poll tax and a literacy test as requirements for voters in all elections. This denied the vote to almost all Mississippi blacks and to many poor whites. Without the federal government to counter this movement, between 1895 and 1910, South Carolina, Louisiana, North Carolina, Virginia, Alabama, Georgia, Oklahoma, Tennessee, Texas, Florida, and Arkansas all enacted similar laws that disfranchised most blacks and many poor whites. In each of these states, after such legislation was enacted, there followed a precipitous drop in black voter registration and in the participation of blacks in public political life. The few blacks who persisted in asserting their civil rights were "visited" by the Klan or some other vigilante group. Funds for the Freedmen's Bureau and for other Reconstruction organizations had dried up. Gone were the white Republicans from the North. Instead, Jim Crow ruled the South. Black participation in national Republican party politics lingered on for awhile. For example, as late as 1892, 120 black delegates were reported to have participated in the Republican national convention. But by 1920, this number had been reduced to 27.

In 1893, Reconstruction officially ended when the U.S. Supreme Court declared the Civil Rights Act of 1875 unconstitutional. In reality, this ruling removed from the books a law that had gone unenforced for some time. Although it is difficult to determine the exact timing and causal relations among such events, it is likely that the Supreme Court's ruling precipitated an escalation in the level of terrorism and violence against blacks throughout the nation. For example, in 1895 there were 113 recorded lynchings of blacks in the South; between 1900 and 1914, another 1,079 deaths of blacks by armed mobs were recorded. And between 1915 and 1918, there were 199 reported lynchings of black Americans in the South (Foster, 1954:421). In the North, between 1898 and 1917, the use of blacks as nonunion strikebreaking replacements in labor disputes increased, resulting in scores of race riots in the industrial cities.

With the death of Frederick Douglass in 1895, little resistance to these political and economic events was offered. Indeed, most black organizations came under the leadership of politicians and public leaders who espoused a policy of appeasement towards the tightening web of Jim Crow practices all around them. Perhaps the last blow to Reconstruction came in 1898 when the U.S. Congress declared final amnesty for all southerners who had previously been considered disloyal or rebellious towards the U.S. government.

Political Oppression in the Twentieth Century

In the period between 1900 and 1950, reversing the oppression of black Americans was given low priority by the federal government. As we see in table 4.1, the number of blacks elected to the U.S. Congress from 1901 through the 1950s dropped to a token few. At no time in the history of the nation have more than two blacks served concurrently in the U.S. Senate. Racial discrimination in the North and the West, coupled with Jim Crow laws in the South, drove blacks from the polls and swept away the few black political leaders who had gained public office.

Similarly, blacks were excluded from appointment to the judiciary. For example, between 1901 and 1961 only twelve black judges were appointed to preside over federal or District of Columbia courts. This pattern of racial exclusion was even more extreme in the appointment of judges at state and local levels.

Thus, at the dawn of the twentieth century, blacks faced a torrent of terrorism and political oppression if they chose to express dissent. Or, if they chose to accept the status quo and wait for white America to recognize their worth, they faced racial and economic discrimination.

Such conditions encouraged the ascendance of Booker T. Washington, well-known director of the all-black Tuskegee Institute. Washington spoke out against aggressive black political action and advocated working hand-in-hand with whites toward the common interests of both races. This logic struck a positive chord among most black Americans, who feared for their lives under current conditions. Washington became a popular leader with a tranquilizing effect on the black masses. Consequently, he gained backing and support for his programs from the federal government and northern philanthropists, and controlled the flow of funds from these sources into safe integrationist causes. Token political appointments of southern blacks, too, came to require the approval of Washington. The Tuskegee Movement, as Washington's policies and programs came to be known, flourished during the first half of the twentieth century. Although not holding an elected political office, it was Booker T. Washington who represented most black people in this period.

TABLE 4.1.

Blacks elected to the U.S. Congress by region for each congressional term from 1901 to 1982.

Congressional Term	United States	South	North and West
1901–1929	—	—	—
1929–1931	1	—	1
1931–1933	1	—	1
1933–1935	1	—	1
1935–1937	1	—	1
1937–1939	1	—	1
1939–1941	1	—	1
1941–1943	1	—	1
1943–1945	1	—	1
1945–1947	1	—	1
1947–1949	2	—	2
1949–1951	2	—	2
1951–1953	2	—	2
1953–1955	2	—	2
1955–1957	3	—	3
1957–1959	3	—	3
1959–1961	4	—	4
1961–1963	4	—	4

1963–1965	5	—	5
1965–1967	6	—	6
1967–1969	7	—	7
1969–1971	8	—	8
1971–1973	14	3	11
1973–1975	18	4	14
1982–1984	21	x	x

— represents zero; x indicates data not available.

Source: Saunders, Doris E. and *Ebony* editors (1974); and Government Research Corporation (1982).

Black intellectuals in the North campaigned against Washington's politics of appeasement. W.E.B. Dubois was the most vocal and formidable of the black activist leaders of the time. In 1905, Dubois called a meeting of black leaders at Niagara Falls to organize opposition against racism and Washington's "wait and see" political posture. This meeting inaugurated the Niagara Movement, which lasted about four years and laid the foundation for much of the successful black activism of the 1950s and 1960s. The Niagara Movement lacked funding and critical political support; as a result, its activities were restricted to holding conventions and formulating demands and policies that went unheeded by the government. But the movement provided a much-needed forum for articulation and codification of political issues, and it eventually attracted more support.

In 1909 and 1910, Dubois and his associates from the Niagara Movement met with a handful of northern whites and formed the National Association for the Advancement of Colored People (NAACP). According to Frazier (1957b:525), its program called for "the abolition of all forced segregation; equal educational advantages for black and white children; awarding and guaranteeing blacks the right to vote; and enforcement of the Fourteenth and Fifteenth Amendments." Dubois was elected director of publicity and became the first editor of *The*

Crisis, the organization's monthly newspaper. Slowly but methodically the NAACP waged a battle in state and federal courts against racism in employment, housing, and education.

In 1911 the National League on Urban Conditions, later called the National Urban League, was formed by another contingent of conservative black leaders and their white supporters. From the outset, Urban League policy was conservative and called for avoiding all political controversy. Instead, it concentrated on analyzing and publicizing living conditions among poor blacks in the nation's urban areas. The League helped blacks who had just arrived in northern cities find jobs in industry. It also assisted those with adjustment problems and offered education in social work for a few (Franklin, 1974:330).

The Black American in World War I (1914–1918)

During the period from 1914 to 1918, social issues like racial oppression and injustice in the United States were subordinated because of political events in Europe. World War I was initially unpopular in the United States but very profitable for American industries that supplied Great Britain, France, and other countries with arms and munitions. It was not until April 6, 1917, after several provocative acts by Germany, that second-term President Woodrow Wilson called for a declaration of war.

Franklin (1974:336) tells us that before the United States declared war, 20,000 of the 750,000 men enlisted in the U.S. Army and the National Guard were black. Before the war ended, nearly 2.3 million blacks had registered for the draft and, in all, 367,000 black Americans were drafted and served in the war. Of these, approximately 200,000 were sent overseas. Nearly all were segregated into Jim Crow regiments, and as many as 75 percent of them were used as common laborers (Foster, 1954:432).

In the military, blacks were barred from the marines and the flying corps, and were allowed into the navy only at the lowest levels, usually as servants or orderlies. In the U.S. Army and the National Guard, where most blacks served, racial discrimination was widespread and severe. For example, not until late in the war were black soldiers assigned officers from their own ranks. And when this change was allowed, black officers were trained in segregated surroundings, where they experienced severe discrimination by fellow white officers. In fact, discrimination in the military was so pervasive that in 1917 the NAACP developed a list of demands for black soldiers which included (Foster, 1954:432): the right to serve our country on the battlefield and to receive training for such service; the right of our own best men to lead troops of their own race in battle, and to receive officer's training in preparation of such leadership. These and other demands went largely unheeded by the president and his military administrators. Racial discrimination remained the norm throughout the war and for decades thereafter.

The black soldiers who were stationed at home during the war were regularly subjected to discrimination in housing and training. In many cases, black soldiers were attacked by white townspeople from areas surrounding military bases and then punished by military courts for defending themselves. At every turn, black soldiers were subject to Jim Crow laws and practices. For example, at the end of the war, of 367,000 black soldiers, only three had risen as high as the rank of colonel and two to lieutenant colonel.

Blacks, however, did make significant gains during the war. Like the five middle-ranking successful black officers mentioned above, a minority of blacks made gains in the military and in industry. Indeed, hundreds of thousands of southern blacks fled their homeland and moved to northern industrial cities, where they filled the wartime labor shortage that had been brought about by the embargo on immigration of European laborers. These opportunities afforded many working-class blacks a chance to gain a tenuous foothold in the heated wartime economy of the North.

Life in the Post-War Decade

Despite these gains, blacks faced horrible violence on two fronts after the war. First, black soldiers returning from the war were subjected to the worst atrocities in the South. Be-

tween 1919 and 1922, there were 239 recorded lynchings in
the South, and in 1919 alone, 70 blacks were lynched. Ten of
the victims were soldiers; a few were executed in their uni-
forms. The Ku Klux Klan, which had been dormant for a few
years, experienced a revival. Klan chapters enlisted members
at record rates, spreading north with offices in New England,
New York, Indiana, Illinois, and Michigan.

Second, in the North, yet another kind of violence awaited
blacks. Between 1919 and 1939, labor strikes were numerous
in all industrial sectors, and blacks were often used by industrialists as nonunion strikebreakers. In 1919, the worst postwar
year, twenty-five major race riots occurred as white workers'
resentment against blacks erupted into violence. Many black
workers and their families were attacked and beaten, and much
of their property was destroyed.

It was during this period of heightened violence and una-
bated discrimination against black Americans that the back-
to-Africa movement of Marcus Garvey gained popularity. As
outlined earlier, Garvey believed that blacks would never be
treated fairly in this country and that their only reasonable
recourse was to raise funds for the acquisition of a free African
state and to set up their own all-black social institutions.
Garvey and his organizations emphasized black separatism
and black pride, and they established an armed militia, a prototype of the national army that they would need in Africa.
For awhile, the movement gave hope to thousands of American
blacks who were willing to support any effort to escape the
sea of violence and discrimination in which they were forced
to live. But, with Garvey's arrest in 1922 and his conviction
for illegal use of the mails, the movement lost its momentum
and eventually died.

The Great Depression of 1929-1939

During the Great Depression, blacks lost many of the gains
in employment they had won during the war. Their wages
averaged 30 percent less than those paid whites, and since
they were systematically excluded from most labor unions,
they were typically the last hired and the first fired. It was
these severe economic circumstances, added to the already

heavy weight of social discrimination, that prompted over two million black voters to break ranks with the Republican party in 1932 and vote for Franklin D. Roosevelt for president.

During Roosevelt's tenure as president, blacks realized a few modest gains. For example, the number of blacks employed by the federal government increased, beginning in 1933 and accelerating as World War II approached. Roosevelt was far more willing than previous presidents to meet in public with black leaders. Whereas Frederick Douglass had, on more than one occasion, been disinvited from campaigning for a U.S. president, Roosevelt openly sought the advice and support of influential blacks. But most of the social reforms of the New Deal era did not directly affect blacks. Indeed, the military remained segregated, southern blacks remained almost totally disfranchised, and blacks in the North continued to encounter job, housing, and educational discrimination.

Beginning in 1935, however, and continuing throughout World War II, blacks benefitted from the gains made by labor unions to organize American workers. In 1935, the Committee for Industrial Organization (CIO) split from the AFL, precipitating heated competition between the two unions for membership among American workers. This competition often resulted in strikes during which nonunion black workers suffered heavily, but it also allowed a million or so blacks to join unions. Early on, the CIO adopted a policy of nondiscrimination against blacks, and although there is much evidence that discrimination was common in CIO affiliates, blacks had at least become members. The competition provided by the CIO and its change in racial policy forced the AFL to eventually modify its Jim Crow policies, thereby allowing a minority of black workers into its membership.

In general, the increase in white and black union membership during this period was remarkable. All together, it increased from 3 million members in 1936 to 10 million in 1940, and on to 15 million union members in 1946. Blacks, to a lesser extent, also entered into the union movement. In 1930, it is estimated there were about 110,000 black union members. In 1936 this number had increased to 180,000, and between

1935 and 1948 black union membership swelled to over 1.15 million workers (Foster, 1954:498). These were important gains to a small element of northern black workers, but millions more blacks in the North remained unemployed or underemployed. Unionization of the South lagged far behind the North, as southern blacks still encountered Jim Crow laws and practices.

The Black American in World War II (1939-1945)

In all, more than 3 million black Americans registered for the draft in World War II and over 1 million enlisted in the military, mostly in the army. About 500,000 black soldiers served overseas, with a much higher proportion serving in fighting units than had in prior wars. Yet, at the beginning of World War II, discrimination against black troops was commonplace. Indeed, little had changed since 1917. Black soldiers were segregated into their own fighting units; black officers were ignored by whites and had little authority outside their all-black units.

From 1943 on, however, discriminatory practices in the various branches of the military were relaxed considerably. Although much discrimination persisted, this relaxation improved the general lot of the black soldier. All branches of the service were opened to blacks, and promotions within the bottom ranks became possible. For example, during World War II approximately 6,000 black officers received appointments, though there were still very few high-ranking black officers. Throughout the course of the war only one black brigadier general, ten colonels, and twenty-four lieutenant colonels rose through the ranks of all U.S. military services. Also, most black soldiers, as in other American wars, were confined to service and supply jobs, where they continued to feel the subtle, day-to-day pressure of racial discrimination.

Nevertheless, the partial breakdown during World War II of racial discrimination in the armed forces was an important gain. It made it possible for more black Americans to pursue military careers and they, in turn, have made it a better world for more recent black recruits.

The "Nonviolent" Civil Rights Movement
(1949-1970)

The end of World War II marked the beginning of a brief period of ascendance for black civil rights causes. Beginning in 1946, and extending throughout his presidency, Harry Truman committed the executive branch of the federal government to a course of action that would help blacks make important inroads against racial inequality. Truman spoke out publicly against the isolation and exploitation of black Americans; he appointed integrated investigative panels to look into discrimination; and he was the first president to adopt an official policy of complete racial integration in the armed forces. It was also under Truman's stewardship that all public facilities in Washington, D.C., were, for the first time, desegregated.

Truman's support was important. Combined with a general increase in size of the northern, voting-conscious, black middle class, it made possible a rise in black voter registration. This, in turn, motivated black leaders in the North to seek public office. Consequently, beginning about 1949 and continuing to the present, small numbers of northern blacks have been elected to serve in municipal governments and state legislatures, and a few have served as high-level appointees of the federal government. But this was a slow process that did not produce a large number of black elected officials until after 1964.

In 1949, the NAACP stepped up its legal battles in federal courts to win racial equality in the areas of labor, housing, education, and the use of public facilities. NAACP lawyers often met with success in the federal courts, but their victories there were usually blocked by Congress, by evasive and nullifying local court rulings, and by simple nonenforcement of court rulings. Neither the North nor the South was yet willing to give up the deeply entrenched tradition of excluding blacks.

Several major events in the 1950s seemed to promise even greater political participation for blacks. During the Korean War (1950-1953), large-scale integration of black soldiers into the regular fighting forces of all branches of the U.S. military services occurred. In 1950, the U.S. Supreme Court ruled that it was illegal to segregate blacks on dining cars that traveled on interstate railways. In 1954, the Supreme Court again ruled in favor of blacks in the famous *Brown vs. School Board of Topeka* decision that affirmed the illegality of racial segregation in public schools. In the elections of 1954, black candidates made encouraging gains. Finally, in 1955, the AFL and CIO, the nation's giant labor unions, announced plans to merge and appointed two powerful black labor leaders, A. Philip Randolph and Willard Townsend, as vice-presidents. While this in no way signaled an immediate end to racial discrimination in the policies of affiliate unions, it did mark a turning point toward greater participation by blacks in the American union movement.

Changes in the South. Most of these gains occurred in the North and the industrializing West. Jim Crow laws remained intact in the South, and they showed amazing strength against the assaults of the executive branch and the federal judiciary. In this context of conflict between the federal government and local traditions, it was perhaps inevitable that the voice of protest would once again be heard throughout the South. In Montgomery, Alabama, in 1955, Rosa Parks changed the history of America by refusing to take her mandated seat in the "colored" section of a city bus. In fact, Mrs. Parks refused to give up her seat so that a standing white man could sit down, and as a result, she was arrested. Thus began the protest movement that would shape American politics for over a decade (Abernathy, 1971). In the days that followed, the black citizens of Montgomery rallied around Rosa Parks and organized a successful boycott of the city bus system until it was desegregated. Through the Montgomery boycott and similar successes in other cities, blacks came to realize that political advantage could be gained by organizing to exercise economic power.

Probably as important as the victory itself was the emergence of Martin Luther King, Jr. and Ralph Abernathy as leaders of the "Nonviolent Movement." Ministers of the two leading black churches in the Montgomery area, they came to prominence after organizing the successful 1955 bus boycott. On January 10, 1957, they met in Atlanta, Georgia with other black leaders to organize the Southern Christian Leadership Conference (SCLC). King was elected the organization's first president and Abernathy its secretary/treasurer. That night Abernathy's home in Montgomery was leveled by a bomb blast. The next day, his church, the famous First Baptist in Montgomery, was also destroyed by bomb blasts. Like other political leaders before them, Abernathy and King had been warned not to organize.

Federal Support for Civil Rights. Despite such incidences of violence, the SCLC initiated an immensely successful membership drive and for ten years thereafter organized sit-ins and boycotts for black causes in scores of southern cities. As the Nonviolent Movement gained momentum, support from the federal government increased. This support was necessary because, as SCLC and other new protest organizations increased their activities in the South, a backlash of terrorism and violence ensued against them. For example, beginning in 1957, homicide rates of blacks increased dramatically. Moreover, race riots and violence followed the Nonviolent Movement's every turn. Federal law had successfully put a lid on lynching in the late 1930s. Thus, bombing became the most common and most devastating medium of terror. In reaction to violence spreading across the South, Congress passed the Civil Rights Act of 1957, empowering various agencies of the federal government to bring suit in federal court to protect all citizens' right to vote. The act also created the U.S. Commission on Civil Rights to enforce the first civil rights bill passed by Congress since 1875. The Justice Department also began to put more emphasis on enforcing civil rights laws in the South. Since white southern racism was buttressed by the authority of local courts and police organizations, these moves by the federal government were only partially effective. But the standoff between state and local governments, on the one hand, and the federal government, on the other, allowed the civil rights movement to continue into the 1960s.

When John Kennedy became president in 1960, he was confronted with a renaissance of black political action everywhere in the nation. In the North, for example, Black Muslim organizations, under the leadership of Elijah Muhammed, were opening new offices and attracting members. In 1961, W.E.B.

Dubois gave up on America and, in protest against persistent American racism, renounced his U.S. citizenship and moved to Ghana. Events like these announced a rebirth of black nationalism among the urban masses. To combat unrest among black Americans, Congress passed a strengthened Civil Rights Act in 1960. The act put teeth in the nation's civil rights laws, and it empowered various agencies of the federal government to act in order to protect the right of every citizen to vote. In response to the rash of southern bombings, it outlawed the vandalism of churches, synagogues, and other public buildings. Robert Kennedy, the U.S. attorney general, pledged the resources of the Justice Department to enforce these new federal codes.

For the next three years, John and Robert Kennedy, along with the leaders of the Nonviolent Movement, combined forces under an uneasy, faltering truce to force more social change on the South than had occurred since Civil War days. Kennedy appointed a number of blacks to positions in the federal judiciary; in small numbers, blacks were appointed to other high-level government positions. Robert Kennedy reorganized the Justice Department in order to enforce those laws that prohibited racial discrimination in education, housing, labor, and politics.

The fight began in 1962 when James Meredith, a black man, was denied enrollment at the University of Mississippi. At President Kennedy's direction, U.S. marshals and national guardsmen intervened on Meredith's behalf and, under the threat of military action by the U.S. government, the University of Mississippi was desegregated. This incident precipitated race riots and considerable violence between whites and blacks, but through it all, Meredith stayed in school. In 1963 Governor George Wallace ordered state policemen to block another black student from entering the University of Alabama. Again the federal government intervened, and another major southern university was integrated. Confrontations like these opened many southern public facilities to blacks.

But the leadership of the Nonviolent Movement was not satisfied with the gains that had been made. There was still rampant discrimination in federal government hiring practices and blacks were subjected to intensified white terrorism in the

South. For example, in 1963 Reverend King led a mass demonstration against racism in Birmingham, Alabama during which the marchers were attacked and beaten by white crowds. Rather than arresting the white mobs, local police arrested the demonstrators and charged them with violating the law.

King led a march on Washington on August 28, 1963 in which more than 200,000 citizens demonstrated for more federal jobs and equal treatment for blacks. Not much came of this march, but its impact undoubtedly predisposed many members of Congress to vote in favor of soon-to-be-introduced civil rights legislation. With King unwilling to give up, it appeared that the government would be forced to make further concessions to the vocal black constituency he represented.

With the assassination of the Kennedys and Martin Luther King, Jr., the Nonviolent Movement receded. The gains it achieved for blacks, however, should not be discounted. For example, Thurgood Marshall, a black NAACP lawyer, was appointed to the U.S. Supreme Court in 1967. A few other blacks, like Andrew Young, have since been appointed to high-level offices in the federal government. In 1964, after President Kennedy's death, the U.S. Congress passed the Civil Rights Act that had been prepared by members of his administration.

Changes in Voting and Office-Holding Patterns. A more lasting gain realized by the Nonviolent Movement was passage of the Voting Rights Act of 1964. This law closed the remaining loopholes, like poll taxes and literacy tests, that had been used by southern state and local governments to deny blacks the vote. As a result, the largest numbers of black Americans in history registered and exercised their vote in the presidential elections of 1964 and 1968. Since that time large numbers of black Americans have continued to register, though each term fewer are actually going to the polls.

Increases in voting activity by black Americans have, in turn, helped many black leaders successfully run for public office. Figure 4.1 describes the trend of this progress in recent years. It shows, for example, that since 1964 the number of black representatives in Congress has more than tripled. In 1966, Edward Brooke, a Republican from Massachusetts, became the

first black man since 1874 to serve a full term in the U.S.
Senate. In fact, 1964 was the first time in the twentieth century
that as many as six blacks served concurrently in the U.S.
Congress. As can be seen, blacks have realized even more impressive gains in their quest for state and local offices. Most
notable of all is the growing number of black mayors who have
been elected to office in recent years. As blacks have become
a majority in many major American cities, the reins of government switch to their leaders. This began in 1967, when Carl
Stokes was elected mayor of Cleveland, Ohio, and Richard
Hatcher won office in Gary, Indiana. In 1973 Los Angeles and
Atlanta elected their first black mayors, even though Los Angeles is predominately white. By 1983 over two hundred American cities had black mayors and, correspondingly, an increase
in the number of lesser black officials now serving in municipal
government has also occurred.

Developments Since the Mid-1960s. During the Vietnam
War of the 1960s and early 1970s, black Americans made new
gains in the military services. In 1967, at the height of the war,
there were 302,000 blacks serving in the armed forces, or
roughly 9 percent. In the desegregated military, blacks were
welcome; when the United States converted to an all-volunteer
military system in 1972, new opportunities for blacks to become career soldiers were created. The most recent figures
available show that in 1978 there were still around 300,000
black soldiers in the military, accounting for 14 percent of all
military forces. Each year since then, blacks have registered
for military service in greater proportions than have whites
(U.S. Department of Commerce, 1982). Thus the all-volunteer
U.S. military is becoming an increasingly black military.
    During the late 1960s, there was a brief resurgence of a black
nationalist movement throughout America. For example, in
1967, the Black Panther Party for Self Defense was formed in
California by Huey P. Newton and Bobby Seale. Soon thereafter
Eldridge Cleaver became the leading Panther spokesman.
Chapters of the Black Panthers were formed in many cities
where large numbers of young black males found the tactics
of King and his followers too tame. The Black Muslims, attracted many new members during this period, as did other

Figure 4.1.

Black elected officials by type of office for selected years, 1964 to 1980.

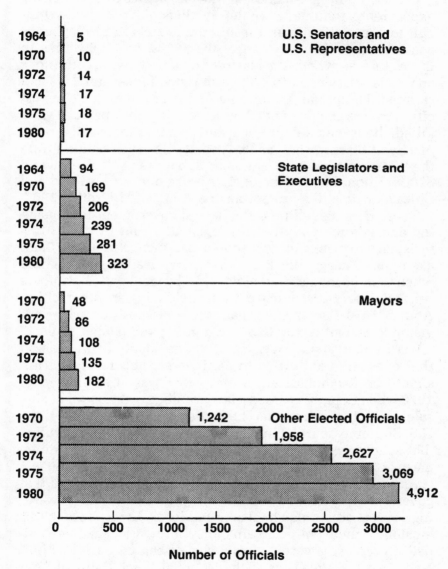

U.S. Senators and U.S. Representatives

Year	Value
1964	5
1970	10
1972	14
1974	17
1975	18
1980	17

State Legislators and Executives

Year	Value
1964	94
1970	169
1972	206
1974	239
1975	281
1980	323

Mayors

Year	Value
1970	48
1972	86
1974	108
1975	135
1980	182

Other Elected Officials

Year	Value
1970	1,242
1972	1,958
1974	2,627
1975	3,069
1980	4,912

Number of Officials

Source: U.S. Department of Commerce, Bureau of the Census (1979), p. 146; and Joint Center for Political Studies (1981), pp. 4–5.

black nationalist groups, although their political influence has receded dramatically in recent years.

One effect of the Nonviolent Movement was to create rising expectations that made the deprivations of blacks more difficult to endure. Partly as a result, urban riots in black ghettos became a prominent feature of the 1960s. In 1965 blacks in the Watts area of Los Angeles rioted over poor living conditions and racial discrimination. The riot lasted for several days and stopped the normal functioning of one of the nation's largest cities. Before the riot ended, at least thirty-four persons were killed, thousands were injured, and over four thousand arrests, mostly of blacks, were made. Property damage resulting from the Watts riots has been estimated at between $40 million and $200 million. In 1966 major riots broke out in Cleveland and Chicago, with still more rioting in Newark and Detroit in 1967.

These riots helped prod the federal government into enacting and enforcing civil rights legislation. But by the 1970s, resistance to black political actions had increased. In 1970, for example, Chicago Black Panther party leaders were killed when their headquarters was attacked by local police. Panthers were similarly discouraged from organizing in other cities. And in 1970 Daniel Moynihan wrote his position paper advising President Nixon to adopt a policy of "benign neglect" toward race-related issues. In 1971 President Nixon ordered that executive activities to achieve school desegregation should be deemphasized, a move that was strengthened in 1972 when Congress passed a law prohibiting the use of busing solely to achieve the racial integration of schools. In 1974, the U.S. Supreme Court joined the antibusing movement by ruling that school systems could not be required to desegregate by means of a comprehensive metropolitan busing program.

As early as 1970, black leaders in Congress recognized that governmental policy had shifted away from the gradual awarding of basic civil rights to black Americans. In response to this erosion of their political gains, they formed a "shadow cabinet" to protest government policies of benign neglect. Similarly, in 1972, delegates at the National Black Political Convention issued protests over government neglect of race-related issues. Yet, the trend was clear: the Ford, Carter, and Reagan administrations avoided race-related issues and let each state develop its own racial policies. As a result, few political gains have been made in recent years.

The Cumulative Legacy and Current Forms of Political Oppression

It is in this general context of historical events that the political power of blacks at the local, state, and national levels of government must be viewed. Despite increases in the registration of black voters and the number of black office holders in recent years, the legacy of the political past, coupled with the present unresponsiveness of the political system to all categories of poor, limits the exercise of black power.

At the National and State Levels

At the national level of political decision making, black powerlessness is, to a great extent, a result of the long history of political disfranchisement. As we have outlined in this chapter, soon after slavery was formally abolished and blacks were legally entitled to vote, a series of informal practices in the South prevented them from registering and voting in large numbers. One strategy was the poll tax, which was enforced against poor blacks and relaxed for poor whites. Another tactic was the use of such devices as the "literacy test" and "constitution test," which again were differentially enforced for blacks and poor whites. When these measures of exclusion were declared illegal, administrative obstruction—long lines, much paper work, elaborate documentation of residents, and the like—effectively kept blacks from registering to vote. And underlying all these techniques was the frequently implemented threat of white violence for "niggers who got out of hand."

Not until the mid-1960s—less than two decades ago—were many of these exclusionary tactics, such as the poll tax and literacy test, finally outlawed. The removal of these roadblocks to voter registration, coupled with growing black political consciousness in all regions of the country, caused racist political strategy to shift from denying the vote to blacks to diluting the impact of their increasing voting power. The most frequent technique of this strategy has been the gerrymandering of congressional districts in order to break up the ghetto and spread its votes into two or more districts where whites can be assured of outnumbering the divided black vote. In this way, very few blacks have been elected to the House of Representatives, and it is only in the last decade that representation has even begun to reflect the actual proportion of blacks in the general population. In senatorial and presidential races, white votes always outnumber black votes, creating a situation where Congress has represented the will of whites and their interest groups—labor unions, trade associations, and large corporations. And again, it is only within the last decade that voter registration in urban areas has reached a level where white candidates must at least pause and consider the "swing vote" potential of black bloc voting.

Even if signs of growing black voting power and representation in Congress can be observed, the effects of nearly two hundred years of exclusion from national politics cannot be easily undone. For example, how can new programs change the apartheid between urban and suburban areas (a pattern of segregation that was the result of federal policies during suburbanization)? Or, how can the effects of forty years of union, employment, and business discrimination be undone as black representation becomes more proportionate? Or, how is schooling to be made more equal in the face of rigid residential segregation and unequal tax assessments to finance schools? Thus, many of the economic, residential, educational, and other key structural arrangements in American society are now so well established that only a massive financial and political commitment to changing them could eliminate the cumulative legacy of past disfranchisement and underrepresentation in the political process. Such a commitment, however, is unlikely because of the present structure of political decision making in America.

Two general features typify the present structure of national decision making in America: (1) an inability to reorder national priorities, and (2) a difficulty in establishing and implementing effective national and change-oriented programs. While there is nothing inherently racist in these features, their existence signals the difficulties of overcoming the past legacy of racism in America, since to change basic institutions would require both a reordering of current priorities and effective national programs. Thus, in a *de facto* sense, the national political system is oppressive for black Americans because it perpetuates the existing structural patterns that have for so long discriminated against them.

Within the congressional branch of national government, at least four structural features preclude a reordering of priorities and the enactment of effective national legislation. One of these concerns the relationship between elected officials and the interests that finance their campaigns. Despite "reforms" in the post-Watergate era, the election process in America continues to be expensive, creating a situation where elected officials, especially at the congressional level, are dependent upon the money of well-organized and financed interests. Since these interests are financially well heeled, they have derived some benefit from the existing system and are therefore resistant to either a reordering of national priorities or to national programs that would alter the existing lucrative institutional arrangements. A second feature of Congress is its vulnerability to lobbying activities of any well-organized and financed group, regardless of whether or not it has helped finance a campaign. Whether a labor union, a trade association, a large corporation, or a department of the executive branch of government (such as the Pentagon), each is able to exert disproportionate influence that usually involves advocacy of existing arrangements and their extension.

A third structural feature of Congress is the seniority system which, despite some recent rule changes in the Senate, places the chair of key committees in the hands of those with more seniority. The result is for many essential committees, through which change-oriented legislation must pass, to be controlled by a chair who is from a stable constituency—typically rural with a southern and midwestern bias—and who is thus more likely to favor the status quo. A final obstacle to the reordering of priorities and effective national legislation inheres in the structure of representative government in a heterogeneous society. Any new, expensive, change-oriented, national program will threaten coalitions of interests that may have conflicts

among themselves but that perceive a threat to their position.
For example, a national program to increase economic equality
will threaten, for different reasons, the Defense Department
(fear of losing money in support budget), labor unions (fear of
losing jobs for current members), and business (fear of government interference in their affairs and profits). While these
individual sectors of the economy may clash among themselves, they have a common interest in stalling any national
legislation that might threaten their particular interests. Similarly, a majority of white Americans of different backgrounds,
regions, states, and cities may have little in common except
their fears about changes in the status quo. So they too exert
influence, again for different reasons, to prevent drastic
changes in priorities and to impede national programs that
might disrupt existing arrangements.

The executive branch of government is subject to these same
four pressures in seeking to either initiate or implement new
programs of national significance. What is more, the executive
branch has the power of enforcing court orders and of implementing congressional legislation with the result that, even if
sound laws of national scope are ordered by the courts or
enacted by Congress, enforcement and effective implementation may be blocked. For indeed, the president is under pressure from unions, business, trade associations, corporations,
and departments of the executive branch to "keep things as
they are" or "extend and expand programs in their current
profile and direction." Probably the most dramatic example of
these pressures and how they impede enforcement and implementation is in the area of civil rights, where again and
again laws pertaining to school desegregation, housing, discrimination, fair employment, and job and union opportunities
have only been partially acted upon by the Justice Department.
With current efforts to dramatically reduce federal spending
under the Reagan administration, enforcement and administration of civil rights codes will become increasingly proble-
matic.

Thus, in looking at the structure of national decision making,
racism is clearly evident. This racism may not be related to
prejudicial attitudes and bigotry, but its consequences for the

lives of black Americans are no less profound: the failure to change the cumulative legacy of institutional arrangements that continue to perpetuate their disadvantaged position.

At the Local Level

At the local community level, similar patterns of institutional racism in the political arena can be observed. While federal policies do indeed affect local political patterns, community political systems have revealed a parallel but autonomous form of racial oppression. In the rural South the same forces—disenfranchisement, poll taxes, eligibility tests, and violence—that kept blacks out of national politics operated even more effectively at the community level since the local white power structure could exert immediate pressure on black residents.

With the urbanization of blacks in the twentieth century, gerrymandering of city wards became an effective tool to keep blacks' representation in city politics low. And when the numbers of blacks in cities began to increase to a point where old gerrymandering techniques would no longer work, a large "black ward" with one representative was sometimes established, with the result that black representatives in city government could consistently be out-voted by the larger number of white representatives from smaller white wards. In the face of this situation, black representatives have been forced to make extensive compromises with the white majority in order to help their communities. Such compromising techniques often bring charges of "Uncle Tomism," but equally often there has been no choice for black representatives who have desired to do at least something for their constituency.

In addition to underrepresentation or ineffectual representation in elected positions of city governments, blacks have encountered even more problems in penetrating the nonelective civil service and patronage positions of local government where much of the actual decision making occurs. One reason for this exclusion was the timing of black migration into the cities. Previous generations of Europeans had used the city political machines not only to secure benefits but also as a path of upward occupational mobility. But by the time blacks began to migrate to the cities, the patronage system had become closed and not easily penetrated by new migrants or, as was the case in many cities, it had been replaced by a civil service bureaucracy dominated by educated whites. In contrast to the political machines, this bureaucracy has been less corrupt, but it has become more detached from, and perhaps less representative of, the people it serves.

With growing numbers of blacks in large cities and with greater numbers of educated blacks who can meet civil service requirements, many of the historical obstacles to black participation in elective and nonelective positions of city governments have been surmounted. But again, the timing of this political ascendancy appears to be operating against blacks, for just as blacks have achieved some degree of political power in the large core cities of metropolitan regions, there are pressures for regional and metropolitan governments. Increasingly, many of the patronage positions formerly run at the city level—planning, health, fire, sanitation, water—appear to be assumed by regional governmental bodies, with the result that they are more likely to be dominated by white suburbanites. While there are sound fiscal and governmental reasons for regional governments, one consequence of their ascendance may be to lessen the number of positions of power and patronage available to upwardly mobile blacks and to give control of many vital services affecting the welfare of blacks back to whites. The end result would be another form of *de facto* racism in which whites residing in the suburbs could conceivably control the fate of large black populations living in the core cities of metropolitan areas.

To the extent that blacks cannot have proportionate political power in the cities, a potential base of power in the national political arena is undermined. The growing significance of the cities in federal fiscal policies—from revenue sharing to mass transit systems—could signal a period of black participation in elective and nonelective bodies in federal, state, and local governments. Yet, such participation is far from proportionate today, and it is not clear that it will become so in the near future with the likely trend toward metropolitan governance. And if black Americans cannot assume some degree of effective political power, their capacity to change racist institutional arrangements in the housing, economic, and educational sectors of the society will be correspondingly diminished. Such is the nature and potential of political oppression of blacks in America.

Summary

In the last few decades the prominence of some black leaders perhaps gives the illusion that black political power is proportionate to the size or needs of the black population. The conspicuousness of these leaders, who emerged primarily in the tumultuous 1960s, has strengthened commitment to "equal opportunity" beliefs about the political opportunities available to all groups of Americans. But as is evident, opportunities are not equal, and even if they suddenly became equal, the current political system reveals little capacity to redress the institutionalization of racism in other institutional sectors.

"Equal opportunity" assumes that no discrimination in occupational positions exists and that people have an equal chance to acquire skills proportionate to their innate abilities. We have seen in the last two chapters that discrimination has prevented, and continues to block, full and proportionate participation of blacks in the economic and political spheres. In the next chapter, we will analyze how the educational system in America has worked to decrease the opportunities for blacks to acquire skills for those occupational positions that could reduce their oppression. For even if we assumed little or no job discrimination in America, blacks are at a disadvantage in acquiring skills that would enable them to take advantage of this situation.

CHAPTER FIVE:

Educational Oppression

Black slaves were, of course, imported into an agrarian society and were used to maintain its plantation system. In such a system, formal education and literacy are not absolutely necessary. But as a society moves from an agrarian form to a more commercial and industrial profile, literacy and other skills acquired in formal educational structures become increasingly necessary for full participation in the economy. Those who fail to acquire these skills will tend to be placed in marginal and often precarious economic and social positions.

During industrialization, educational structures become "gatekeepers" for economic interests. Educational credentials, in and of themselves, become symbolic representations of a general cluster of job-related skills and attributes. And increasingly, educational credentials are used as an initial screening mechanism for placing people in high- or low-paying economic positions. To the extent that a population is denied access to the educational system, or given unequal treatment while in the system, "educational oppression" exists in a society, since the lack of "credentials" will systematically exclude members of a population from access to a society's scarce and valuable resources.

113

The history of black Americans' involvement in educational structures is one of open oppression. Initial efforts were directed toward exclusion of blacks; when this was no longer possible, segregation into inferior schools became the typical strategy. Even today, despite impressive gains by blacks, educational oppression still operates in American society. In this chapter, we will attempt to portray the varying forms that this oppression has taken during the history of white-black relations in America.

Pre-Civil War Forms of Educational Oppression

It is likely that some blacks were formally educated in the great Muslim cities of West Africa. But for the most part, the 6.2 million blacks who were captured in eighteenth-century West Africa and exported to other parts of the world as slaves had lived in outland villages, where no written language existed and where education involved word-of-mouth teaching and the apprentice method of learning. Of the nearly 700,000 slaves counted in the 1790 census in America, most came from West Africa. Around 200,000 were believed to be under ten years of age. From this we surmise that probably less than 2 percent of the black slave population could read and write (Weinberg, 1977).

Conflicting reports exist about the extent to which slaves were educated by white owners in eighteenth- and nineteenth-century America. Some authorities say that an early affinity developed between large numbers of slaves and their owners, with the result that many slaves were taught to read and write. Others contend that slaves were treated more like domesticated animals, with only a necessary few achieving literacy.

We do know that in 1740 South Carolina was the first state government to adopt a compulsory ignorance law for slaves. This law read, in part:

> And whereas the having of slaves taught to write, or suffering them to be employed in writing, may be attending with great inconveniences;

Be it enacted, that all and every person and persons whatsoever, who shall hereafter teach, or cause any slave or slaves to be taught to write, or shall use or employ any slave as a scribe in any manner of writing whatsoever, hereafter taught to write; every such person or persons shall, for every offense, forfeit the sum of one hundred pounds current money (Weinberg, 1977:13).

Such laws emerged in all southern states and counties until the 1860s, when they were swept away by the Civil War. In each southern locality, ignorance laws were worded somewhat differently and prescribed varying penalties for violations. Moreover, their enforcement appears to have been irregular, though swift and effective in many cases.

Despite enslavement and compulsory ignorance laws, many blacks sought education. Secret schools operated everywhere in the South, although they were least common in the most oppressive states, like Alabama and Mississippi. Yet, in other places such as Charleston, South Carolina, the Society for Propagating the Gospel operated a regular segregated school for blacks as early as 1774 (Helm, 1909:136).

Though few in number in the pre-Civil War South, free blacks fared somewhat better than their enslaved counterparts. Some southern free blacks were educated in segregated public schools. Others were taught through a variety of means, including secret schools, private schools, church schools, and apprenticeships. In 1850, literacy among southern free blacks in non-Deep South states ranged as high as 43 percent in North Carolina to a low of 20 percent in Virginia. No such estimates are available for the Deep South, but it is believed that literacy was far less common there, even among free blacks.

There were isolated instances where blacks were educated in open schools. In culturally elevated spots throughout the South, a handful of such schools for blacks existed before the Civil War. For example, Helm tells of fifteen such schools, paid for by blacks, operating between 1800 and 1861 in the District of Columbia. Records indicate that in North Carolina there were also many such schools for blacks. Another free school was run openly from 1819 to 1829 in Savannah, Geor-

gia, and secretly for a time thereafter. In Maryland, black Ro-
man Catholic sisters opened the "St. Francis Academy for col-
oured girls" in 1829 (Helm, 1909:136). In Virginia, in 1764, a
Williamsburg newspaper editor operated a school for blacks.

In the North, one of the earliest schools for blacks was established in 1704 in New York City by the Society for the
Propagation of the Gospel. This school was run by Elias Neau,
a pious man who approached the teaching of letters through
religious instruction. Another early northern school for blacks
was run in Philadelphia by Quakers, with its doors opening
in 1770 and remaining open well into the twentieth century.
Another such school was initiated and supported by black
parents in 1798 in Boston (Helm, 1909:135). In 1820, black
parents in Cincinnati established their first school, with other
such schools soon following throughout Ohio. An uncommon
practice occurred in New Bedford, Massachusetts, where
schools from their beginning were open to black students.

Even though educational opportunities were much better in
the North, schools were not universally open to blacks, nor
was the quality of their education typically equivalent to that
received by whites. In many respects "separate and unequal"
was the model pattern in the North long before it became the
policy of southern school districts. As is the case today, the
separation of whites and blacks was the result of residential
segregation. In turn, residential segregation resulted from acts
of white violence against blacks who were perceived as an
economic threat by poor whites. Indeed, industrial capitalists
were often interested in using, or threatening to use, black
labor as a way of keeping white workers' wages low. White-
black tensions created a climate of fear, often reinforced by
white violence (and less often by black reprisals). For example,
the early 1800s in Philadelphia were typified by intense pressure from black parents and the Quakers to open the public
schools for blacks. Such pressures were countered by sporadic
violence against blacks, culminating in the 1830 riots. The
result was suspicion and fear on the part of blacks entering
white areas of town, to say nothing of white schools (Weinberg,
1977:21). Another example of the educational barriers to
blacks comes from Boston in the 1880s. In response to intense

pressure from black parents, the city government eventually created schools for blacks that were clearly inferior to white schools in terms of physical facilities and personnel. Similarly, in Connecticut and Rhode Island a combination of white violence and deliberate school segregation created a dual system of education.

At the higher education level, there were few educational opportunities for blacks before 1865. The first black university was established in 1854, when Lincoln University in Pennsylvania opened its doors to a few students. The second came two years later when Wilberforce in Ohio admitted some students. The first nonblack college to admit blacks in large numbers was Oberlin, which one year after its founding in 1833 began to admit black students. Indeed, historically and to this day, Oberlin has a distinguished record of leadership in the higher education of young black men and women (Brawley, 1929:105).

In sum, then, prior to the Civil War educational opportunities for blacks were few. In the South, blacks were systematically excluded from educational structures, whereas in the North their inclusion into the emerging educational system was on a less than equal basis with whites. Thus, at the dawn of the Civil War, young blacks received virtually no education. Since the slave population had been growing by reproduction rather than importation, a large cohort of blacks would not have the skills necessary to take advantage of increased economic opportunities during the brief period of Reconstruction following the Civil War.

Educational Oppression after the Civil War

During the Civil War, most schools in the South were closed. In the North, where a longer tradition of public education existed, and where towns and cities were free from military invasion, the schools remained open, but maintained the inequalities of the pre-war day. Yet, in both the North and the South, the post-war era saw the full institutionalization of free public education for all children and the establishment of a dual system for white and black children (Cash, 1941:3–102).

This profile of education in America has remained essentially unchanged until recent years.

In the South before the war, there had been an emerging system of public instruction for white children. But this system was destroyed by the war, as were the few schools for southern blacks that had existed. Out of these ashes emerged a new system of education, part public and part private, for both races. The first southern schools for blacks after the war appear to have been in military camps, with students meeting after the workday ended. Teachers were most often blacks who had achieved a modicum of literacy and who were willing to pass along their limited knowledge to others. Teachers and students alike usually worked at another job and attended classes in off-work hours. Students in the same class often ranged in age from extremely young children to "gray-beards." Thus, students of all ages and ability levels could be seen working together, unbound by slavery for the first time in nearly two hundred years.

The Work of the Freedmen's Bureau

In 1865 the U.S. Congress created the Freedmen's Bureau. Initially the bureau was charged with providing food, clothing, and shelter for black and white southern refugees who flocked to Union army camps. But in 1866, Congress changed the enacting legislation and instructed the bureau to work with groups of black citizens and other private organizations in the South to employ teachers, provide instructional materials, and help teachers acquire educational housing. In the ensuing years, the Freedmen's Bureau spent approximately $5 million in federal monies helping establish schools for black southerners. However, because the bureau's activities were limited to the larger southern cities, only a minority of blacks benefited. For example, as late as 1870, approximately nine of every ten black children attended no school at all (Weinberg, 1977:43). Still, the Freedmen's Bureau at least inspired free blacks to create their own schools and provided needed monies. As schools were established in this manner, they became models of others to come, thereby creating a ripple effect.

The Work of Religious Societies

Another important early stimulus to the building of a school system for southern blacks was provided by northern philanthropists and four large religious societies. The largest of these was the American Missionary Association, which had been established before the Civil War and was originally interdenominational. In its formative years the association was organized to abolish slavery in the South and was the first northern religious organization to begin educational work in the South by opening a school for blacks in Hampton, Virginia, in 1861. Taken over by the Congregational church in 1881, in subsequent years the association established an institution of higher education in each of the larger southern states. Under the support of the American Missionary Association, many of the better private southern black colleges emerged, including Hampton University in Virginia, Atlanta University in Georgia, and Fisk University in Tennessee. The association also opened normal (elementary) and graded schools in larger southern cities and built common and parochial schools in rural areas.

The American Baptist Home Mission Society began educating black southern refugees in Union Army camps in 1862. In its early work, the society focused largely on religious instruction, but eventually, as the demand for education among free blacks swelled, the society established a chain of schools that continued to grow until the 1930s. From the late nineteenth century to 1930 the society supported many private schools, and also owned and operated nine institutions of higher education (Brawley, 1929:137). A smaller group, the Freedmen's Aid and Southern Education Society, was organized by northern Methodists in 1866, and by 1930 this organization had built and supported twenty-four southern schools. Finally, for some time after the Civil War, many Presbyterian groups worked independently to educate southern blacks. In 1882 their activities were merged to form the Board of Missions for Freedmen of the Presbyterian Church in the United States of America. This organization, like that of the Methodists and others, stressed religious instruction. The Presbyterian Board of Missions was active especially in North Carolina, South

Carolina, and southern Virginia, establishing institutions of higher education, academies, and parochial schools for blacks.

Despite the diversity of these educational efforts, the illiteracy rate remained high among most southern blacks. The magnitude of the problem was simply too great. Also, southern blacks were nearly everywhere terrorized by whites who feared and opposed their education. If they were caught possessing books or sending their children to school, black parents were commonly threatened with physical abuse by organized groups of white southerners. Frequently, new southern black schools were burned to the ground and teachers were beaten or run out of town. Thus, the tide of white resistance to education for blacks served to minimized educational progress realized in private schools. Throughout the South, ambitious or "uppity" blacks were beaten, and many were hanged or burned at the stake as examples of what would happen to those who pushed for equality with whites. In the minds of most nineteenth-century white Americans, blacks were seen as threatening, and it was believed they should be kept away from white children in public schools.

The Public School System

Between 1870 and 1880, the basic structure of the U.S. system of public education was formed. In the North, state legislatures long before 1870 had begun enacting compulsory education laws and providing funds for public schools. As we noted earlier, "separate and unequal" public schools were the most common result of northern legislative action. In the South, Weinberg reports that the reform minded legislatures of the late 1860s enacted compulsory education laws for blacks and whites, while providing funds for free universal education. Yet, although the southern state legislatures provided some funding for public schools, most funding came from local property taxes, with the result that the schools were controlled from the outset by local community school boards. Thus, between 1870 and 1880, several factors, including the end of slavery, public school legislation, and the beginning of a national system of public education, attracted large numbers of new black students to public schools. In fact, the ensuing increase in school attendance by black children was great. Weinberg estimates that, by 1880, one-third of all black children in the United States were enrolled in public schools (1977:45–54). But this did not result in their being educated equally.

By 1880, the political tides had begun to turn against blacks, especially in the South. Black parents everywhere discovered that they were required by law to pay taxes in support of public schools, even though most were segregated and their children were excluded. Where public schools for blacks were required by law, black parents were usually required to pay taxes to support dual educational systems; little public tax support was forthcoming from local white governments for black schools. In many political jurisdictions in the South, public schools for whites were required by state and local law, but schools for blacks were "voluntary." As a result, they were not supported by public funds at all. As we will see, between 1880 and the present, this problem grew worse. More and more black children, both in relative and in absolute terms, have sought public schooling, but the common pattern of education has been to isolate black children in segregated and inferior schools. Indeed, between 1870 and 1905 the sixteen southern states spent one-fourth as much for black schools as was spent for white schools.

During this period in American history, it was generally believed by whites and blacks alike that black children needed only the most basic literacy training. Black common (elementary) and high schools tended to emphasize achieving literacy and acquiring a basic work skill. Throughout the South, especially between 1885 and 1930, industrial training was also favored by private black universities such as Hampton and Tuskegee. Though the curriculum varied from school to school, the main work of these all-black industrial schools consisted of "training men and women who can in turn train industrially the great mass of people in private and secondary and in the public schools of city and country" (Helm 1969:146). In 1902, Gibson and Crogman estimated that eighteen such schools existed in the South, in which industrial education was given in carpentry, tinning, painting, plastering, shoemaking, tailoring, blacksmithing, farming, and gardening.

By 1900, the southern industrial schools had produced 1,243 graduates working in the following occupations: 693 teachers, 117 ministers, 163 physicians, 116 lawyers, 5 editors, 15 merchants, 36 U.S. government service employees, 12 farmers, 2 mechanics, and 1 carpenter (Gibson and Crogman, 1969). The importance of such training for southern blacks was great, but it obviously involved only a small fraction of the total number of southern blacks in need of education and training.

Another aspect of the emerging pattern of public education for blacks in nineteenth-century America resulted from urbanization. Before the Civil War, rural southern blacks had begun to migrate in large numbers toward southern cities like Atlanta and Charlotte. Urbanization greatly accelerated for a twenty-year period directly after the war for several reasons. First, industrialization around southern cities attracted large numbers of blacks who could not find work on the reconstructed farms and who had heard that work was available in the new factories of the urban South. Second, many black parents seemed to believe that urban public schools would provide greater opportunities for their children than the nonexistent or viciously racist rural schools. Although the process of black urbanization abated considerably during the last two decades of the nineteenth century, the population of blacks living in major southern cities before the turn of the century increased by as much as three-fold (Weinberg, 1977:64). It seems that by moving to southern cities, black parents did achieve somewhat better educational opportunities for their children. For example, available evidence indicates that, on the average, urban southern school systems spent more money, per capita, educating black children than did the majority of rural southern schools. Yet, moving to southern cities did not guarantee equal or even acceptable education for black children. They still attended separate, vastly inferior schools relative to whites.

In sum, then, the system of public education for black Americans that emerged after the Civil War represented an improvement over education under slavery, but this system was horribly inadequate. By 1890 illiteracy among American blacks had shrunk from almost 100 percent in 1790 to approximately

60 percent. At the same time, however, blacks everywhere in the United States had been shunted into another America; they were forced to live a ghetto life and their children were condemned to education in run-down, segregated city schools. This pattern had initially emerged in the North, but in the post-Reconstruction era, it also became institutionalized in the South. By the turn of the century, the system of public education for blacks in the North and the South was not dramatically different.

Educational Oppression in the Early Twentieth Century

The early decades of the twentieth century saw an increasing urbanization of black Americans, with the result that their children would be educated in urban public school systems. Yet, close to one-half of all blacks in the 1920s and 1930s still lived in the rural South; as a result, they received an even more inadequate education than their urban counterparts.

Increasing Black Participation

Despite many problems and failings that we will discuss shortly, black Americans began to participate actively in the educational system, albeit unequally. Tables 5.1 and 5.2 document this participation in two ways. First, table 5.1 reports the number and percentage of school-aged blacks and whites who participated in the school system. Second, table 5.2 compares the decline in illiteracy rates for blacks and whites. When viewed in a positive light, the data show a dramatic decline in black illiteracy and a sharp increase in school attendance. When viewed more negatively, black illiteracy in 1930 was six times that of whites and even in 1969 was four times the level for whites. And it was not until 1975 that black school enrollment reached parity with white enrollment.

These data tend to underemphasize the disparities between blacks and whites in several ways. First, the definition of literacy is extremely lax in that only the rudiments of reading and writing are necessary to declare a person "literate." Thus, the data do not report the degree of literacy, which is, on the

average, much greater for whites than blacks. Second, enrollment figures do not fully represent the vast differences in the
quality of schools in which students are enrolled. Again, on
the average, whites attend schools of much greater quality than
blacks.

The Urban School System

The most profound aspect of educational oppression during
the first half of the century was the creation of the dual educational system. The hallmark of this system was, and still is
today, the large, segregated city public schools. For example,
Weinberg reports that Phillips High School in Chicago was the
first large, segregated school in the area. In 1921 its enrollment
was 75 percent black and 25 percent white. By 1930 there were
at least twenty-six such schools around Chicago in which 85
percent or more of the students were black (1977:69). To take
another example, in 1913 black children accounted for only

TABLE 5.1.

**U.S. school enrollment, selected years, 1890–1980
(numbers in thousands).**

Year	Total	Black Enrolled Number	Black Enrolled Percent of total	Total	White Enrolled Number	White Enrolled Percent of total
1890	2,998	987	33	18,140	10,454	58
1940	4,389	2,837	65	32,742	23,456	72
1960	6,624	5,225	79	44,329	36,439	82
1975	8,670	7,507	87	52,092	44,961	86
1980	8,746	7,871	90	56,448	50,238	89

Source: U.S. Department of Commerce, Bureau of the Census (1979a), p. 88;
U.S. Department of Commerce, Bureau of the Census (1982), p. 20; and U.S.
Department of Education (1982), p. 9.

TABLE 5.2.

**Illiterates in the U.S. population 14 years old
and over, by race, selected years, 1890–1979
(numbers in thousands).**

	Black		White	
Year	Total	Illiterate	Total	Illiterate
		Percent of total		Percent of total
1890	4,259	61	35,818	8
1930	8,027	18	77,357	3
1969	14,280	4	127,449	1
1979	18,337	1.6	148,965	0.44

Source: U.S. Department of Commerce, Bureau of the Census (1979a), p. 91;
and U.S. Department of Commerce, Bureau of the Census (1979b), p. 17.

about 4 percent of the public school enrollment in New York City. By the 1930s this population had increased dramatically, with the result that overcrowding became a serious problem. The inadequate curriculum in black schools, the use of discriminatory reading materials, the deliberate attempts at school segregation, and the openly discriminatory practices against black teachers had emerged as publicly acknowledged problems throughout the city school system. These problems were so serious that the mayor, Fiorello La Guardia, appointed a committee, headed by black sociologist E. Franklin Frazier, to study racial discrimination in Harlem. Though the committee had little impact and its reports were largely suppressed, it found widespread discrimination in the New York City public school system. A report of the 1935 Frazier committee said:

> The Negro in Harlem has made serious complaints against the schools of the community on the grounds that they are old,

poorly equipped and overcrowded and constitute fire hazards.
. . . The welfare of the children is neglected and racial discrimination is practiced. . . . It seems that many of the white teachers
appointed to the schools of Harlem regard the appointment as
a sort of punishment. . . . The problem of education is the same
as all other problems: Namely, to make the same educational
provisions for the school children of Harlem as are made for
children in other parts of the city, and see to it that Negro
teachers are admitted to all branches of the teaching staff (Weinberg 1977:73).

The Pattern of Segregation

This pattern of public school segregation developed everywhere in the United States between 1920 and 1940. In the
South, racial isolation in public schools was openly encouraged by state and local legislatures, by the courts, and by local
school boards. In the North it was commonly believed that
blacks attended substandard segregated schools not because
legal authorities intended it to be so, but because most blacks
lived in segregated inner city areas and therefore attended
segregated schools by necessity. Although the North has
proved more hospitable for many blacks, *de jure* and *de facto*
school segregation have been commonly practiced everywhere
that blacks have migrated in the twentieth century. Throughout the country, economic forces and legal authority have isolated blacks residentially and educationally (Banfield, 1970;
Weinberg, 1968).

In the South, many laws existed prohibiting blacks from
living in certain sections of towns and cities; school assignment was segregated and openly based upon race. In the North
and the West, fewer residential segregation laws existed, but
black housing was nevertheless segregated; school assignment
was supposed to be based upon residence rather than race,
that is, the laws required that children attend schools in prox-
imity to their residence, but in reality school assignment was
based upon residence and race. When blacks lived close to
segregated, run-down schools, their assignment by school
boards and courts was based upon residence, and they were
forced to attend local, segregated schools. When blacks lived

closer to modern, predominantly white schools, their assignment was most often based upon race, and they were forced to attend more distant, segregated schools.

Antisegregation Actions

During this period the forces against educational segregation were mobilizing. A minority of blacks throughout the country had gained stature in business, religion, law, and government; and slowly, they had organized to push the government for more gains. Moreover, liberal whites began a renewed effort to redress the problems and grievances of black America. And, as the nation's courts ruled in the 1950s that more and more blacks had the legal right to vote, support for large organizations like the National Association for the Advancement of Colored People and the Urban League grew. Such organizations petitioned the government to certify the rights of black children to equal education. The most noteworthy of these activities was carried out by the NAACP's Legal Defense Fund in 1954 in *Brown v. Board of Education of Topeka*. A black man, Thurgood Marshall, who was later to become an Associate Justice of the U.S. Supreme Court, argued before the Court that black parents in South Carolina, Virginia, Delaware, Kansas, and Washington, D.C., had been "deprived of the equal protection of the laws where the statute requires appellants to attend public elementary schools on a segregated basis, because the act of segregation in and of itself denies them equal educational opportunities which the Fourteenth Amendment of the U.S. Constitution secures."

In a surprise decision, the U.S. Supreme Court unanimously ruled in May of 1954 in favor of the NAACP, but there was no strong provision in the Court's ruling laying out a timetable for school desegregation. As Marshall had warned the Court, without such a timetable, state legislatures, local courts, and school boards would find it easy to delay action on correcting educational racism by citing the myriad "complexities" they must first overcome. Thus, the *Brown v. Topeka* decision set a legal precedent in favor of equality of educational opportunity, but until the 1960s, the court's decision was ignored by most American school systems (Stent, 1979:81).

Educational Oppression after the Brown Decision

The U.S. Supreme Court decision in *Brown v. Topeka* (1954) was a turning point in the educational history of black Americans. It marked the first time a powerful agency of the federal government had taken a stand against school segregation. And, since the Supreme Court is the highest and most powerful judicial body in the nation, it must have seemed plausible to blacks that local school boards would at last heed their petitions for admission to white schools. Throughout the nation, but especially in the South, black parents put this assumption to the test by petitioning local school boards on behalf of their children, for admission to white schools. Almost all local school boards reacted in the traditional manner by rejecting the petitions for one or another reason. The most common reasons for rejection were black parents' failure to complete complicated special admission applications and the failure of their children to "pass" newly devised compulsory admission tests or interviews. These new strategies devised by local school boards to repulse black children came to be known as "pupil placement laws," and they became, according to the U.S. Commission on Civil Rights, the "principal obstacle to desegregation in the South" (1962:4).

Slow Progress

Where the rejected petitions were taken to court by black parents, local and state courts almost always ruled in favor of the local school board. Since appeal through the federal court system is time consuming and costly, few of these cases were taken into higher courts on appeal. Those parents who did persevere into higher federal courts, however, often won. But Stent reports that, from 1954 through 1960, it was not uncommon for state legal systems and local school boards to ignore the direct orders of a federal district court, especially when its intent was to enforce the Brown decision (1979:81).

Black parents who openly petitioned southern schools for acceptance of their children were caught in a bind. On the one hand, they had been encouraged to pursue equal education for their children by the Supreme Court and by their own predominantly black political organizations. On the other hand, the Court had difficulty forcing its will over the strong tradition of southern racism. Equally significant, black efforts to enter white schools generated new and escalated antagonisms that led to increased discrimination. For example, the fifty-seven black parents in Orangeburg, South Carolina who in 1955 had petitioned the local board to eliminate school discrimination were fired from their jobs. They were denied credit and access to food; and in some cases they were thrown off the land they sharecropped. A similar fate befell the activist parents of black children in Yazoo City, Mississippi where the NAACP had presented the local board with complaints filed by fifty-three black parents. Here, too, parents were fired, families went without food, and black children and parents were beaten. Before long, all fifty-three parents had withdrawn their complaints (Weinberg, 1977:90-91; Stent, 1979:80-81). This process was repeated in many places in the South, and in fact, Weinberg reports that as many as two years after the Brown decision, no black children were attending white schools in Alabama, Florida, Georgia, Louisiana, Mississippi, North Carolina, South Carolina, and Virginia (1977:91).

Throughout the 1950s, Congress was kept out of the southern desegregation issue because of the efforts of powerful southern congressmen and their allies to block legislation whose aim was educational reform. Congressional unwillingness to help blacks was based at least in part on the fact that blacks had never before voted in large blocs in national elections. Thus, there was no incentive to come to their aid.

In the North during the 1950s, desegregation also progressed slowly. Urban black children attended segregated schools in run-down buildings, with limited materials and inferior teachers. In Philadelphia, for example, between 1956 and 1963 the proportion of black children in predominantly black schools (over 80 percent black) increased from 72 to 85 percent. In New York City, from 1955 to 1965, the number of predominantly black and Puerto Rican schools increased from 52 to 201 (Weinberg, 1977:102).

Thus, the Brown decision was an important turning point, but it resulted in little immediate educational reform. In the

1960s, however, blacks practically everywhere in the United
States won the right to vote in federal and local elections.
Consequently, black voter registration in urban areas increased
rapidly. Sensing this change in the character of the voting
public, some members of Congress began to change their position on the desegregation issue.

Factors Favoring Desegregation

A convergence of factors set the stage for the next event in
the history of black public education in the United States. First,
as we have already noted, black activism accelerated throughout the 1950s and 1960s. At the forefront were Reverend Martin
Luther King, Jr. and the NAACP. In all parts of the country,
Reverend King led concerned people in sit-ins, marches,
prayer meetings, and straight talk about the obvious oppression of black people by white institutions. Through the
NAACP, philanthropic monies were channeled into federal
and local legal battles against widespread segregation. Second,
in the early 1960s, changes in the makeup of federal government went well for prodesegregation forces. John F. Kennedy,
a liberal Democrat, was elected president of the United States
in 1960; and from the congressional elections of the same year,
a new wave of more liberal representatives came to Congress.

Another factor in favor of desegregation was the makeup of
the Supreme Court during the Kennedy-Johnson era. Though
the Court is always conservative, at its head through the 1950s
and 1960s was Californian Earl Warren, who favored extending
constitutional rights to all U.S. citizens. Thus, for a brief period
in history, all three major branches of the federal government
tilted in favor of school desegregation for blacks and other
minorities.

Two other converging factors were less central to the growth
of the federal desegregation movement of the 1960s. Yet they,
too, were important. First, the United States economy was
rebounding from the severe recession of the late 1950s. Industrial growth and political/military activities in Southeast
Asia, South America, and elsewhere helped the economy gain
strength at an unprecedented rate. The heated economy gen-

erated large federal tax revenues, and for a brief period of time, the federal government had extra funds that could be diverted to domestic reform.

Finally, the general affluence of the white working and middle classes in the United States in the late twentieth century favored desegregation. As is often the case in such periods of prosperity, education and the arts prospered and there was a liberalization of attitudes.

The Civil Rights Act of 1964

From this convergence of forces, the major event of the 1960s was passage by the U.S. Congress of the 1964 Civil Rights Act. The act was comprised of eleven titles, ten of which are summarized by Weinberg (1977:121-22):

Title 1. Strengthened the federal role in prevention of racial discrimination in voting.

Title 2. Outlawed racial discrimination in public accommodations engaging in interstate commerce.

Title 3. Gave the U.S. attorney general, the president's brother Robert Kennedy, the right to sue to desegregate public facilities.

Title 4. Empowered the U.S. commissioner of education, an appointee of the president, to help school districts to desegregate, and the attorney general to institute lawsuits to force desegregation of schools or colleges.

Title 5. Enlarged the powers of the U.S. Commission on Civil Rights to conduct inquiries.

Title 6. Forbade the racially discriminatory use of federal funds in any federally assisted program.

Title 7. Created the Equal Employment Opportunity Commission to outlaw job discrimination because of race, color, religion, sex, or national origin.

Title 8. Directed the U.S. Department of Commerce to supply the Commission on Civil Rights with current statistics on registration and voting.

Title 9. Regulated the authority of the attorney general in prosecuting certain cases involving equal protection of the laws.

Title 10. Created the Community Relations Service, to help resolve community disputes based on race, color, or national origin.

President John F. Kennedy, whose administration submitted the Civil Rights Act to Congress, was assassinated in Dallas in 1963. He was succeeded in office by Lyndon Johnson, the liberal vice-president from Texas. Robert Kennedy, the U.S. attorney general, remained for a while in the White House, as did other Kennedy liberals. In 1965 the U.S. Department of Health, Education and Welfare issued guidelines spelling out how the Civil Rights Act of 1964 should be implemented. Simultaneously, however, powerful opponents of the act in Congress moved to block its implementation. The HEW guidelines of 1965 emphasized Title 6 of the act, which prohibited the use of federal funds to underwrite educational programs that were discriminatory.

Between 1965 and 1967, the use of economic incentives by HEW forced many large southern school systems to desegregate. This pressure resulted in a significant decrease in all-black schools in many southern communities. But local school boards also took advantage of the situation by firing black principals and black teachers as schools were closed. Thus, the legal activities of the federal government resulted in some mixing of school children in the South, but also caused a reduction in the number of black teachers and administrators.

Social Research Studies

One consequence of the desegregation movement of the 1960s was a factual glimpse at the extent of racial isolation in the public schools and at the character of the black-white achievement gap. Two major social research studies of educational racism are worthy of note in this context. Title 4 of the Civil Rights Act of 1964 required that the extent of inequality of educational opportunity among blacks, other minorities, and whites be studied nationally. This was done in 1965 and 1966 by the U.S. Office of Education under the direction of an academic researcher, James Coleman, from Johns Hopkins University. In its 1966 Equality of Educational Opportunity (EEO) survey, the U.S. Office of Education studied characteristics of student populations, teachers, and facilities among a sample of American public schools. Of particular interest is their analysis of differences in black-white performance on standardized verbal ability and reading achievement tests. EEO researchers recognized that such achievement tests do not always accurately measure innate ability and are far from free of cultural bias. "What they measure are skills which are among the most important in our society for getting a good job and moving up to a better one, and for full participation in an increasingly technical world" (Coleman, 1966:20).

The EEO survey found blacks in metropolitan areas lagging behind their white counterparts at all levels of schooling. Blacks start school with less verbal ability than whites (Coleman, 1966:221). At the sixth-grade level, blacks, on the average, are approximately one and one-half years behind white children in verbal achievement. At the twelfth-grade level, blacks, on the average, are performing at just below the ninth-grade norms, while whites are performing at just below the twelfth-grade level (Coleman, 1966:273-74). The study concluded that public education remains largely unequal in most regions of the country, including all those "where Negroes form any significant proportion of the population." Moreover, the great majority of American children attend schools that are largely segregated—that is, almost all of their fellow students are of the same racial background as they are (Coleman, 1966:3).

The second important study, commissioned by Congress and the president in 1965, was performed by the U.S. Commission on Civil Rights in 1966 and 1967 with the help of a large panel of social scientists. In its letter to the president, which accompanied the commission's report, the panel declared that the study substantiated the president's belief "that racial isolation in the schools serves as a deterrent to the full development of the country's human resources" (1967:iii).

This report concluded that "levels of segregation are discernibly higher in the South than in the North, [but] the two regions [of the nation] do not fall into discrete categories." In fact, "the extent of racial isolation in northern school systems does not differ markedly from that in the South" (1967:7). The commission found school segregation severe in the nation's major metropolitan areas, where most blacks and whites currently live, with the most extensive isolation in inner-city areas, where "nine of every ten Negro elementary school students attend majority-Negro schools"(1967:5). In general, in the seventy-five cities studied by the commission, "75 percent of the Negro students are in elementary schools with enrollments that are nearly all-Negro (90 percent or more Negro), while 83 percent of the white students are in nearly all-white schools" (1967:3). Perhaps the most disturbing finding of the commission was that population growth among blacks in metropolitan and inner-city areas was likely to continue throughout the century. Thus, increases in racial isolation are likely.

These major social science studies on the extent and consequences of racial isolation in public schools documented what was already known: in most cases blacks across the nation attend segregated schools and, on the average, their accomplishments fall far short of white student performance. These findings fueled the flurry of school desegregation of the late 1960s, aided in large part by federal court rulings and congressional mandate. More recently, however, congressional and judicial sentiment in favor of desegregation has cooled, especially since the 1974 Supreme Court ruling that the fifty-three districts that comprise public education in the incorporated suburbs of Detroit could not be compelled to merge with the city of Detroit's schools in order to achieve racial balance (Weinberg, 1977:84).

The extent to which racial isolation still exists in American public schools is difficult to determine. As the government's goals and policies have changed, relevant data have become difficult to obtain. Nevertheless, it appears that fewer American children are in totally segregated schools, especially in the Deep South. But the available evidence also indicates that too little has been done to erase the achievement disparity between black and white students. Table 5.3, for example, shows the percent of Americans between fourteen and seventeen years of age, by race, who are two or more years behind modal grade level in 1950, 1960, 1970, and 1977. The table shows that with each decade proportionately fewer blacks and whites lag two or more years behind in school. But well into the 1970s over twice as many blacks as whites were performing two or more years below modal grade level.

TABLE 5.3.

Percent of enrolled persons 14 to 17 years old who are two or more years below modal grade level by race: 1950, 1960, 1970, and 1977.

Race	1950	1960	1970	1977
Black	52.3	31.8	21.1	6.8
White	21.1	12.6	9.0	2.9

Source: U.S. Department of Commerce, Bureau of the Census (1979a), p. 90; and U.S. Department of Education (1980), p. 15.

In table 5:4 the percent of high school dropouts among persons between fourteen and thirty-four years of age is shown by race for October 1980. This table shows that high school dropout rates remain much higher for blacks than whites. Dropout rates are especially high for young adult blacks. Thus, the available data indicate that racial isolation, despite considerable governmental intervention, remains common in American public schools and that blacks, on the average, benefit less than whites from school attendance. In fact, the proportion of blacks in 1980 who are twenty-five years and older and who have less than five years of elementary school education is three times higher than for whites. Similarly, blacks are less likely to have graduated from high school than whites, and blacks are much less likely to have spent four or more years attending college than are whites of the same age.

Summary

The history of black involvement in American educational institutions has entailed attempts at exclusion. When outright exclusion became impossible, segregated inclusion has been the most prevalent pattern. These discriminatory forces have had a profound effect on the plight of black Americans. In a society that relies heavily upon educational credentials for

TABLE 5.4.
Percent of high school dropouts among persons
14 to 34 years old by race, October 1980.

Race	Total 13–34 years	14–15 years	16–17 years	18–19 years	20–21 years	22–24 years	25–29 years	30–34 years
	1	2	3	4	5	6	7	8
Black	18.8	2.0	16.9	21.2	24.8	24.0	22.6	23.5
White	12.1	1.7	9.2	14.9	14.5	13.9	12.7	13.4

Source: U.S. Department of Education (1982), p. 68.

placing and promoting people in the occupational sphere, the educational system assumes great importance in determining the chances of individuals to participate in American affluence (Berg, 1971; Ellis, 1971).

The Educational Dilemma in America

While the correlation between level of educational attainment and income has declined somewhat in recent years, post-high school education is still related to income potential and access to other scarce resources, such as power and prestige. Yet, educational credentials, even from colleges and universities, do not assure occupational success for minority populations (Jencks, 1972). Despite a dramatic increase in black college enrollments, it is not clear that increased levels of education will be translated, proportionately, into escalated income, primarily because of discrimination in other institutional spheres. Even worse off are blacks who fail to complete high school, complete high school with severe deficiencies, or complete high school but do not continue their education. These categories of blacks will be even less likely than their college-educated counterparts to gain access to scarce resources.

To some degree the failure of blacks to achieve educationally, especially in the sense of real acquisition of abilities (rather than credentials that are often given to students without much regard for ability), is not the result of educational discrimination. Class position for both blacks and whites is inversely related to educational attainment. Since blacks are overrepresented (because of past and present discrimination in the economy) in the lower classes, they are less likely than middle-class children to exhibit those skills that facilitate real (as opposed to credential) performance in schools, whether segregated or integrated. Moreover, many of the learning difficulties of lower-class blacks stem from a combination of family, neighborhood, and peer relations that do not encourage or train students for academic performance (again, these are related to patterns of economic, political, and housing discrimination).

The real dilemma in American education, then, revolves around the extent to which the educational system can overcome the legacy of past and present discrimination in other institutional spheres. To what degree can the schools overcome such problems as: (1) housing discrimination and the problems of slum and ghetto life; (2) job discrimination and the related problems of poverty and personal frustration of parents; and (3) family pathologies, such as parental dissension, dissolution, and divorce, that stem from 1 and 2 above.

It is questionable whether a large, publicly funded bureaucratic system like the schools could ever develop the requisite flexibility and sensitivity to deal with the problems of black students. And it is most unlikely that this system can effectively deal with these problems in light of its historical involvement in racial oppression. But even if we assume that the past legacy of blatant discrimination would suddenly cease, there are more subtle patterns of discrimination in schools that are more difficult to eliminate.

How does lower education in America still discriminate? Until recently, the most readily apparent form of discrimination was school segregation. As commentators had long argued, and as the Supreme Court reaffirmed in 1954, segregated schools were rarely equal in terms of physical facilities, textbooks, libraries, work plans, classroom size, and teacher qualifications. The EEO Report (Coleman et al., 1966) confirmed many of these assertions, although regional and social class differences in the quality of schools were often as marked as racial differences. Furthermore, to the surprise of some, the differences in black and white educational achievement as measured by grades and standardized test scores was less influenced by the actual physical and programmatic characteristics of the schools than by students' social class and family background, the nature of their peer interactions, and the characteristics of teachers (1966:259).

Maintaining the Status Quo

While the EEO data reveal that blacks in integrated schools attain higher levels of achievement than their counterparts in segregated schools—presumably because of more "favorable" peer interaction and teacher characteristics—one of the problems with the EEO Report and other such studies is the implicit acceptance of the current culture and structure of American education. For example, to assess achievement, the existing measures of performance—grades and test scores—are employed. While these procedures cannot and should not be totally discounted, they are simply an extension of a more general practice in American schools: to teach, evaluate, and sort black students in terms of methods and procedures constructed and implemented by whites for white students. In many ways, the EEO Report reaffirms the more subtle and yet equally profound racism in public schools: the acceptance of the system the way it is, and the conviction that it is necessary and desirable to force blacks and other minorities into white schools where they can be "exposed" to learning styles and performance criteria that now place whites at a competitive advantage. And since textbook writers, test makers, school administrators, and classroom teachers are more likely to employ white, middle-class cultural criteria in the performance of their respective tasks, students of lower-class and minority cultural backgrounds will be more likely to encounter "learning" and "achievement" problems. Such cultural bias marks a subtle and yet profound form of discrimination.

The structure of schools responds to a great extent to the demands of an economic system dominated by successful whites. As long as school performance bears a strong relationship to placement in the job market, it can be expected that the schools will continue to give the managerial classes in the economy "what they want." To be properly qualified and thereby acquire a "good job," both blacks and whites must have demonstrated a level of performance as confirmed by an educational credential, in a school system expressing and personifying white managerial preferences. But a critical question needs to be asked: Are these criteria of educational performance really necessary for satisfactory performance in most jobs? It seems doubtful that this is the case, for most jobs in the economy require little formal training, and what specific skills are involved can usually be acquired on the job. Thus, from one point of view, the schools legitimate the racial oppression evident in the job market by placing an overemphasis on conformity to interpersonal styles, methods of learning, performance criteria, and accrediting procedures that favor "achievement" by whites and "learning problems" for blacks.

One pattern of educational racism, then, is the implicit acceptance of current hiring and promotion practices existing in the job market. By ignoring the deviations of black American culture from white middle-class culture, the educational system subtly discriminates. It is not surprising, therefore, that the EEO Report and others have found class, family, and peer factors to deter educational achievement in schools dominated by white middle-class cultural premises. For indeed, cultural deviations should be highly associated with class, family, and peer socialization experiences. The key question is: Is the family or peer group "culturally deprived" or is it the school with its middle-class patterns that is deprived? It would be incorrect to place the entire burden of failure to achieve on the schools, for there may be "learning problems" associated with poverty and isolation from the mainstream of society. But does the school exacerbate these problems by rigidly imposing middle-class standards on young students from diverse cultural backgrounds? To the extent that the schools do, then they are as oppressive as the other institutions in the society that have perpetuated the disadvantaged position of blacks.

Common Features of School Systems

While the details of school organization vary somewhat from area to area, there are certain common features that typify the vast majority of schools and school systems in America (Turner, 1972:179-90). Many of these features are subtly discriminatory in that they do not adequately meet the emotional and learning needs of children and adolescents from nonwhite cultural backgrounds. First, American schools are highly bureaucratized, with an emphasis on classroom orderliness, conformity to rules, clear "lesson plans," extensive record keeping on student performance, and clearly articulated relations among teachers, students, and administrators. While relations between students and teachers appear on the surface to be

casual and informal, there is a considerable degree of bureaucratic constraint to what, when, and how subject matter is to
be communicated to students (Goodland, 1969). Such a structure can be imposing upon students who do not respond well
to a high degree of formalization in the communication of
subject matter (see, for example, Kozol, 1967). While we must
be careful in drawing premature conclusions about white-
black cultural differences—lest stereotypical beliefs be perpetuated—there appear to be cultural differences between the
expressiveness, spontaneity, and perhaps interpersonal styles
of black and white children, with the result that black children
are often placed in a structure that is alien to their prior experiences. All children face an adjustment to bureaucratic
forms of organization, but the formality of the school structure
is more likely to pose an adjustment problem for black than
white students.

A second endemic feature of the educational bureaucrati-
zation of American schools is their organization into a strict
hierarchy, with the rapid and uneventful passage of students
from one grade to another being the main goal of teachers and
administrators. The passage up the educational hierarchy is
accompanied by constant evaluation of students' ability and
progress. American students are incessantly subjected to bat-
teries of tests. Such tests are defined as competitive endeavors,
with students being rewarded, grouped, and partially segregated in terms of their performances. An emphasis on time,
scheduling, competition, and successful test-taking presup-
poses that students are interested in placing their self-esteem
in, and in concentrating their energy on, a written and cog-
nitively oriented task that appears to have little immediate
relation to their daily lives. Furthermore, the tests themselves
tend to portray a white middle-class world, with the images,
vocabulary, and conceptions of performance of middle-class
test-makers subtly woven into the substance of the examina-
tions (Turner, 1972:206).

For black children, the substance and the necessary test-
taking style can be alien and repulsive, with the result that
their performances during their early years will not be high.
Also, because the rewards of the school system hinge upon

successful test performance, black students are more likely to remove themselves emotionally from the prospect of test-taking failure—a withdrawal of their self-esteem that will place them in "slower ability" groups in integrated schools and, in both integrated and segregated schools, will cause even more withdrawal from alien requirements. It is perhaps for this reason that differences in achievement test scores for blacks and whites increase with movement up the educational hierarchy, since blacks are more likely to retreat from a reward system that increasingly gives advantages to whites who were less alienated by their initial exposure to the system.

Third, the substantive knowledge communicated to students revolves around white culture and history (Sloan, 1967; Marcus, 1961; Knowles and Prewitt, 1969:47-53). As a result, black students are fed a vision of the world that is at odds with, and alien to, one that they have experienced. Coupled with the omission of teaching about black achievements, plus an incredibly benign and patronizing portrayal of black-white relations in America, it becomes increasingly difficult for black students to relate to a white educational world that has little existential meaning—thereby making more likely their emotional withdrawal from all phases of the school's intellectual life.

Fourth, the bestower of knowledge—the teacher—can further alienate black students from the educational system. As a number of studies have documented, teachers (even when they are black) not only communicate a white, middle-class interpretation of the world. They also impose middle-class expectations on their students about how "good" students act, learn, perform, and relate—standards that are more likely to estrange blacks (and lower-class children in general) and thus put them at a disadvantage in competing with white students for the teacher's favor (Rosenthal and Jacobson, 1968; Gottlieb, 1964; Kirkman, 1966; Rist, 1970). The result of this estrangement from teacher expectations and the inability to compete successfully against whites (in integrated schools) is to further accelerate black emotional and intellectual withdrawal from the school system.

Such an educational system is legitimated by dominant be-

liefs about "equal opportunity" that consider the school system as the principal vehicle for the disadvantaged to improve
their station in life. Since schools are free to all and since they
employ "neutral" and "fairly administered" measuring in-
struments of ability and performance, the failure to perform
in schools is seen as the fault of the individual. Even when
more liberal environmentalist beliefs about the detrimental
effects of "cultural deprivation" and "cultural impoverishment" on minority poor are invoked to help account for performance and achievement failure, the presumption is that the
existing school structure can "compensate" for these "background problems" by exposing black students to "white culture." Rarely is the structure of the school system itself, and
the cultural biases built into this structure, seen to be as harmful as are the presumed states of cultural impoverishment
among minority poor. Thus, beliefs sustaining the myth of
equal opportunity and the compensatory capacity of the
schools to overcome black cultural deprivation legitimate a
long established system of oppressive education in America.

Summary

Structural and cultural biases in American schools against
black children and all other children from non-middle-class
backgrounds are clearly evident. The schools in America subtly discriminate against most categories of working and lower
class students, while favoring most middle-class students.
(Turner, 1972:205). Since blacks are situated predominantly
in the working and lower classes, the class bias alone works
against them. When this bias is compounded by the white
cultural biases, then the estrangement of many black Americans from a system that personifies patterns of residential segregation and that reinforces their impressions of white oppression in other institutional spheres is not surprising. Given the
current "necessity" for documented performance in the educational hierarchy if one is to be "successful" in the occupational sphere, these class and cultural biases become translated
into a subtle and yet profound pattern of institutional oppression. Eliminating this oppression represents an enduring
American dilemma.

Structured Discrimination: An Overview

In these last three chapters, we have sought to document the forms of economic, political, and educational discrimination experienced by black Americans. It is in these three spheres that "success" in America is measured, for if a population is to gain access to power, prestige, and material well-being, it must receive proper educational credentials and use these to enhance access to jobs in the economy and government. As we have seen, it has been difficult for blacks to receive either the credentials or the job opportunities necessary to avoid oppression. Such has been the structure of oppression in America.

We noted in chapter 2 that structural arrangements that endure, especially those that are oppressive, must be legitimated by cultural beliefs. Yet, in a complex society, legitimated structural patterns must also be supported by formal laws and agencies of social control. For mediating between the structure of oppression and general beliefs are the laws, courts, and police. Oppression can only be maintained when these three facets of the legal system operate in ways that sanction and support discrimination. As we will see in the next chapter, such has been the case for the oppression of black Americans.

CHAPTER SIX:

Legal Oppression

Dominant values and beliefs, as well as prominent structural arrangements, are typically codified into explicit laws. In turn, these laws are enforced by the state. And once codified and enforced, the law bestows legitimacy on institutional arrangements, thereby making them resistant to change. As we will see, so it was with beliefs about black Americans. Periodically, patterns of discrimination were codified into law. Formalization into laws of discriminatory beliefs and behaviors, however, presents only a partial picture of racial oppression, since informal discriminatory practices against black Americans have often gone uncodified but nonetheless enforced. Moreover, there are situations that are highly discriminatory and yet do not violate the law. For example, housing discrimination is currently forbidden by law, but in light of the economically depressed situation of blacks, coupled with their isolation in urban ghettos (both the result of *de jure* and *de facto* practices of the past), widespread exclusion of blacks from white suburban housing is inevitable, even if it could be assumed that no informal discrimination in the housing industry currently occurs.

There is, then, a complex and subtle set of relationships

among beliefs, actions, and formal laws. Despite these subtle-
ties, the most remarkable historical feature of the American
legal system is that it has openly condoned and legitimated
racial discrimination.

Early Forms of Legal Oppression

Whether the first blacks in America were slaves or indentured servants is difficult to determine, for the historical record
is not clear on this point (Franklin, 1974:56; Jordan, 1962). By
the 1650s, some colonies enacted laws that distinguished between white and black servants, with blacks and their offspring
consigned to servitude for life. Whether these early laws codified existing practices or were enacted to facilitate the man-
agement of the growing slave population can never be known.
We suspect that both forces were probably operating. As a
result, the broad legal framework of slavery in the South had
become clearly codified by the early eighteenth century
(Starobin, 1970:7; Stampp, 1956). This framework embraced
the following tenets:

1. Blacks were to be slaves for life.
2. Slaves were both property and persons, with owners
   holding title to blacks as property but, at the same time,
   having some responsibilities to them as persons.
3. Children would inherit their mother's status.
4. Christian baptism did not automatically lead to freedom.
5. Marriages between blacks and whites were prohibited.
6. Blacks could not acquire or inherit property.
7. Blacks could not engage in litigation or enter into civil
   contracts, nor could they testify against whites in court
   or sit on juries.

Virginia was one of the earliest colonies to enact a slave
code, and it appears to have become a model for other states.
Franklin (1974:58) reports, for example, that the Virginia slave
code, which itself was based on earlier codes worked out by
Caribbean states, imposed the following restraints on liberty:

1. Slaves could not leave plantations without written permission.
2. Citizens were required to return runaway slaves to their rightful owners, or face stiff criminal penalties.
3. Slaves convicted of murder or rape were to be hanged.
4. For major law violations, such as robbery or assault, slaves were to be given sixty lashes; they were to be confined to a pillory; and it was prescribed that their ears be cut off.
5. For minor law violations, such as associating with free blacks or whites and insolence, whipping, branding, and maiming were recommended as suitable penalties.

These laws were enforced by local sheriffs and courts as well as by the military. On or near plantations, such laws were enforced by slave owners, slave managers, and poor whites. Punishment was often administered without the benefit of trial or due process. In this context, the first white vigilante or "night-rider" groups emerged as an important part of the enforcement system that kept blacks in line.

Such codes and their rather harsh enforcement reflected and at the same time reaffirmed beliefs about the "bestiality" of slaves who, because they were "less than human," were not to be treated as full-fledged citizens. These southern codes also legitimated the economic imperatives of slavery by making it appear right and proper that all whites could buy and treat slave labor much as one might do with domestic animals. In the North, the legal codes were considerably more benign than those in the South, but few people questioned beliefs about the inferiority of blacks or the necessity for excluding them from full economic, educational, and political participation (Litwack, 1961:30–38).

With the admission of border and southern states to the Union in the early 1800s, a considerable debate ensued in Congress over the "legal rights" of blacks. The coexistence of free blacks, who possessed at least a few rights (these varied by state), and enslaved blacks, who had virtually no legal rights, presented a problem of how to define the constitutional

rights of blacks in the growing nation. The problem was effectively avoided in 1821 when Missouri was admitted to the
Union, for Congress enacted a vague platitude that allowed
the states to legislate as they pleased, while giving the appearance that no citizens "shall be excluded from the enjoy-
ment of any of the privileges and immunities to which such
citizen is entitled under the Constitution of the United States."
Thereafter, until the Civil War, northern laws were increasingly relaxed, while southern legislatures passed ever more
restrictive laws.

These restrictive codes legitimated the institution of slavery,
while at the same time codifying the proslavery doctrine of
the antebellum South. In the North, abolitionists' pleas for at
least "humane treatment" of "the inferior race" were beginning to have a small impact on public opinion. As a result,
those states having few black residents began to accord them
broader citizenship rights. However, these formal laws con-
tradicted informal practices that prohibited access by most
blacks to jobs, education, and housing. Thus, at the dawn of
the Civil War, formal laws corresponded with discriminatory
practices in the South, whereas the law did little to undo
informal discriminatory practices in the North.

While the Civil War was ostensibly fought over the issue of
emancipation, it appears more likely that the abolitionist ideology was used ex post facto to justify a massive Northern
invasion of the South for economic and political reasons.
Whatever the complex relationship between the Civil War and
abolitionist ideology, the war abolished forever the institution
of slavery and thereby altered dramatically the economic base
of the South. In 1866, these facts were formally ratified in the
Thirteenth Amendment abolishing slavery.

In reaction to the Thirteenth Amendment, southern states
immediately began to enact "black codes" restricting the rights
of "free" slaves. The details of these codes varied enormously
from state to state, but several restrictions on blacks were common to all: (1) blacks could not vote; (2) they could not serve
on juries; (3) they could not testify against whites; (4) they
could not carry arms; (5) depending upon the state, they could
not enter certain occupations; and (6) black vagrants could be
consigned to forced labor. For example, the legislation that

reinstated the black codes in Mississippi after the Civil War required:

> that all the penal and criminal laws now in force in this State, defining offenses, and prescribing the mode of punishment for crimes and misdemeanors committed by slaves, free Negroes or mulattoes, be and the same are hereby reenacted, and declared to be in full force and effect against freedmen, free Negroes, and mulattoes, except so far as the mode and manner of trial and punishment have been changed or altered by law. (W.E.B. Dubois, 1935:177)

The Mississippi law, as an early piece of "black code" legislation, provided a model for other southern states as they drafted legislation to legally restrict the civil rights of the newly freed black population (Frazier, 1957a:126). Thus, in the immediate aftermath of the Civil War, the South was unified in its attempts to impose new legal restrictions upon blacks, thereby perpetuating their servitude in a somewhat altered form.

In reaction to these "black codes" and President Andrew Johnson's rather conciliatory approach to Reconstruction in the South, Congress began to assume control of Reconstruction under the Radical Republicans. While the details of the maneuverings between Congress and the president are extensive, compounded by midterm congressional elections in 1866 and the attempt to impeach Johnson in 1867, Congress eventually became veto-proof and thus initiated its own program of Radical Reconstruction. The Radicals in Congress assumed a two-front legal attack on racism in the South: (1) the division of the South into military districts and the enforcement of new constitutional conventions on each southern state; and (2) the passage of the Fourteenth and Fifteenth Amendments, which were ratified by northern and reconstituted southern states in 1868 and 1870, respectively. The Fourteenth Amendment was an extension of an earlier civil rights act (vetoed by Johnson and then overridden by Congress) designed to overrule the emerging "black codes." The Fifteenth Amendment extended suffrage to blacks. Under Radical Reconstruction, constitutional conventions of southern states were necessary for a state to be readmitted to the Union by Congress. The threat of non-admission and restrictions on who could vote in ratification elections resulted in state constitutions that opened opportunities for blacks in politics, jobs, and schooling. These reforms in the South were soon followed by the Civil Rights Act of 1875, which outlawed northern Jim Crow practices.

In this way, Congress forced the South, and to a lesser extent the North, to accept black participation in key institutional sectors. Had Radical Reconstruction persisted for several generations, racial oppression in America would have been markedly reduced. However, informal violence against blacks, plus changing state and national political conditions, worked against Radical Reconstruction from its beginnings. By 1880, the Radical Republicans had lost control of Congress and the presidency. And in the 1890s, the Supreme Court legitimated the re-emergence of Jim Crow practices. First, the Supreme Court declared unconstitutional the Civil Rights Act of 1875, thus condoning the denial of blacks' access to public conveyances and amusement facilities used by whites. Then, in 1896, the Supreme Court ruled that segregated facilities for blacks and whites were not in violation of the Thirteenth and Fourteenth Amendments since, as the court declared: "If one race be inferior to the other socially, the Constitution cannot put them on the same plane" (Pinkney, 1969:28).

These decisions merely reflected common practices and public attitudes that were rapidly elaborated into an ideological defense of segregation. To codify exclusionary and segregationist practices in the highest laws of the land gave added support to the culture and structure of racism in America. In many ways, these Supreme Court decisions represented the enactment of new "black codes" under the guise of Jim Crow, for exclusion and segregation in housing, recreation, and transportation were easily extended informally to jobs and politics.

Legal Oppression in the Twentieth Century

It was under the burden of this national legal legacy that black Americans entered the twentieth century. During this period, blacks were to become increasingly urban as they began a series of migrations out of the South in search of industrial jobs in the North. In the North, a myriad of discriminatory laws in housing, unions, jobs, and government were to prevent black integration into white institutions and black participation in American affluence. Such laws were not considered illegal or immoral by most segments of the society as they were legitimated by key decisions of the Supreme Court and reflected the post-Civil War belief that blacks had been given a chance and had demonstrated their inferiority. Even when these decisions were subsequently reversed, informal practices of discrimination in housing, jobs, education, and other critical spheres were to persist, since they were supported by widely held beliefs about black inferiority. Once practices and beliefs have been supported by legal codes for a prolonged period, a sudden change in the content of laws does not necessarily lead to corresponding changes in structural arrangements or beliefs. This is particularly likely when the new laws themselves go unenforced. In the twentieth century, blacks have had to struggle against not only the formal legal barriers but also the informal practices of discrimination that have been sustained by the long tenure of these legal barriers. This fight has been primarily against discriminatory laws in housing, jobs, politics, and education—the key institutional sectors blocking equal participation of blacks.

Legal Discrimination in Housing

Since people's place of residence determines, to a great extent, their access to jobs and schools, legal barriers to attaining equal housing have had profound consequences for black Americans. Housing discrimination in America has involved a complex pattern of *de facto* and *de jure* processes that periodically have become codified into law, thereby affirming beliefs about the necessity for isolating inferior races and giving impetus to informal practices of segregation.

In the early 1900s informal practices of housing discrimination were considered proper in light of dominant beliefs and the earlier Supreme Court decision proclaiming that "if one race be inferior to the other, socially, the Constitution cannot put them on the same plane." In this cultural and legal milieu,

the first black migrants to northern cities were forced not only
by their meager resources but also by threats of white violence
and landlord policies into the decaying cores of the cities.
While the wartime industries of World War I provided many
jobs and while the geographical concentration of cities allowed
easy access from the ghetto to work, a pattern of residential
isolation of blacks was initiated that persists to the present
day and that has had profound consequences for blacks' access
to jobs and education in a suburbanized society. This pattern
of segregation was often formalized in communities by restrictive covenants that forbade integrated neighborhoods. During
the 1930s, when economic opportunities vanished in the North
and elsewhere, black migration to the cities waned. Yet it was
during this lull in black migration that the federal government
enacted legislation that was to forge the current profile of urban-suburban apartheid in America.

The most significant piece of federal legislation was the act
creating the Federal Housing Authority and the FHA mortgage
loan guarantee program. By allowing as little as 10 percent
down and by guaranteeing banks payment of the outstanding
mortgages should they fall into default, the act enabled white
Americans to purchase single-family dwellings in the growing
suburbs of large cities. In the post-World War II period, the
FHA (and the related Veterans Administration) mortgage guarantee program stimulated the rapid flight of white Americans
from the cities to the suburbs. Black Americans, however, were
prevented from joining whites by the explicitly discriminatory
administrative rules of the law. Until 1950, for example, the
FHA manual proclaimed: "If a neighborhood is to retain sta-
bility it is necessary that properties shall continue to be occupied by the same social and racial social classes." From 1950
to 1962, when President Kennedy finally issued an executive
order to the contrary, the practice of providing FHA and VA
loan guarantees primarily to white neighborhoods continued.
Even after 1962, FHA policy was "ineffectively integrationist."
Thus, federal law subsidized white housing in the suburbs,
while openly preventing blacks from sharing in the subsidy.

The consequences of this housing law, however, extended
beyond residential segregation. As the American population

began to move from the cities to the suburbs, industry and commerce began to follow. Later, industry began to pull residents out of the cities as new assembly-line techniques, with their need for large tracts of land, increasingly came to dominate the productive sector of the economy. And as industry and workers moved out of the city, commercial and service industries followed. Job opportunities in the expanding economy became available to whites who were allowed to move into the suburbs, but less so to blacks trapped in the cores of large cities. Some blacks could commute out to these jobs, but as mass transit services in America began to deteriorate in the post-World War II period, commuting became even more difficult.

With growing suburbanization the tax base for financing city schools vanished, with the result that suburban schools flourished and urban schools with heavy concentrations of black students languished for lack of financial resources. Suburban communities with large populations of white residents began to exert enormous political power in metropolitan and state-wide governmental bodies, thereby reducing the power of big city governments at the very time blacks began to enter the urban political arena. Thus, urban-suburban segregation, as created by FHA laws, has had profound consequences for blocking blacks' access to jobs, quality schools, and political power. Coupled with the cultural and personal pathologies of impoverished ghetto life in the slums of America's large cities, blacks have been denied access to those institutions that would allow them to share in American affluence.

To cope with the squalor of urban slums, other federal laws have been enacted, but they have not eliminated slum conditions and, more importantly, they have exacerbated patterns of segregation. One of the key legislative acts of the New Deal initiated the public housing program that by 1937 had acquired the social purpose of eliminating substandard housing. Unfortunately, changes in the law in the late 1930s turned the administration of public housing projects over to the cities, with the result that housing projects were built in existing slum areas, thereby perpetuating black confinement to the core city. Urban renewal was another major attempt to revitalize slum areas and to restore the decaying downtown areas of cities in an effort to attract middle-class suburbanites back to the city. But the result of the program was to destroy slum housing and force the poor into public housing projects where few wished to live. "Model Cities" programs have done somewhat better, but they do not attack the basic problem: urban-suburban segregation.

A recent Supreme Court decision has made even more difficult the breakdown of urban-suburban segregation. In 1973, the Supreme Court ruled that suburban communities do have zoning control over patterns of land use in their communities. The result of this ruling has been for local suburban governments to alter the zoning of land tracts in ways designed to keep public housing or federally subsidized home ownership programs for blacks out of the suburbs. Such "zoning-out" techniques have been common practice for a number of years. For example, in Milpitas, California, the land for a union's black housing tract was suddenly rezoned "nonresidential"; and in Deerfield, Illinois, the land for an integrated housing project was condemned for park use. The recent Supreme Court ruling thus legitimizes these housing policies in much the same way as earlier Supreme Court rulings legitimated discriminatory laws and practices.

In the 1960s, Congress enacted a civil rights act that prohibited discrimination in either the rental or sale of housing. Real estate brokers were also enjoined from discrimination, and subsequently the Supreme Court ruled that even individual sellers cannot discriminate in the sale of their own property. While these laws reaffirm "equal opportunity beliefs," they are ineffective in counteracting discrimination, because (1) they often go unenforced (since the Civil Rights Division of the Justice Department is understaffed and underfinanced), and (2) they place the burden of litigation on the individual against whom discrimination has occurred—a personally and financially arduous process.

More importantly, the laws do not attack the fundamental problem: the need for mass migration of blacks to the suburbs where better schools and job opportunities are located. Of course, any such mass policy will encounter the resistance of local communities which, under the 1973 Supreme Court ruling, can zone-out government-sponsored housing for blacks. One of the legal ironies of housing laws, then, is that from the mid-1930s until the mid-1960s, whites were given mortgage subsidies by FHA and VA to move out into the suburbs en masse, whereas current laws prevent a similar mass exodus of blacks. And while FHA and VA laws are no longer discriminatory, they were visibly so at the crucial time of mass suburbanization in America. Thus, while these laws are now benign, they do not eliminate the legacy of past discrimination that created urban-suburban segregation.

Current Supreme Court rulings prevent massive federal programs of integration of blacks into suburban life, forcing integration of the suburbs to occur on a slow, individual by individual basis. Current housing laws—despite their lofty civil rights tenets—continue to perpetuate segregation in housing. As a consequence, they also promote de *facto* discrimination in economic, educational, and political institutions. In a subtle and yet profound way, current laws affirm "equal opportunity" beliefs by "explaining" the absence of blacks in the suburbs as a result of their failure to avail themselves of "equal" educational and economic opportunities that would allow them to buy a house there. Of course, such beliefs underemphasize the fact that past discrimination has forced many blacks to live in the "wrong" neighborhood, attend the "worst" schools, and have qualifications for only the most "menial jobs."

Legal Discrimination in Jobs

Legal legitimation of discrimination in other institutional spheres has been prevalent, even without the exacerbating impact of residential segregation. As we noted in chapter 3, practices in the economy have involved discrimination in lending capital for businesses, in providing job opportunities in the open labor market, and in allowing membership in trade unions. Such practices have limited occupational achievement by blacks. For our present purposes, the important point is that these practices were tacitly condoned by the absence of laws to the contrary. Because of the Supreme Court's suspension of the Thirteenth and Fourteenth Amendments in the last century, job discrimination was allowed to prevail well into this century.

In the 1930s, some discriminatory practices—such as differential wage scales for blacks and whites on WPA projects—were eliminated under political pressure. But it was not until after World War II that clear and enforceable antidiscriminatory laws were enacted. And even these laws were not federal and hence national in scope. Rather, they were enacted on a state-by-state basis, with some states such as New York enacting a tough Fair Employment Practices Law in 1945, but with others failing to enact any antidiscriminatory laws whatsoever. In fact, it was only in 1964—one hundred years after the Civil War—that a strong civil rights act on job discrimination was passed by Congress. While considerable enforcement and voluntary compliance to this law is now in evidence, much informal and illegal discrimination still occurs.

Current fair employment laws do not compensate and significantly address the question of how to correct for over a century of legalized job discrimination. Instead, the law simply forbids present and future discrimination, ignoring the fact that much of the damage has already been done by past discrimination. For many blacks who are trapped in urban slums, who live in unstable families, and who attend inferior schools, there is virtually no chance that they can evidence the skills necessary to secure and hold a job, even should one be available. Such is the legacy of legal inattention to job discrimination.

Legal Discrimination in Education

In education, a similar form of legal neglect has allowed segregation of blacks and whites in unequal schools. Such segregation was compounded by the fact that there were few federal education laws, especially compulsory education codes. Indeed, educational matters have traditionally been left to the states, with many states only recently enacting compulsory education laws. Thus, not only were blacks segregated by law. They were not even required by law to come to school. In fact, the laws often worked to discourage black school attendance.

Only with the 1954 Supreme Court decision outlawing *de jure* segregation of schools (the question of *de facto* segregation has yet to be completely resolved) did the federal government legally intervene in school system activities. And as the post-1954 record reveals, even this Supreme Court decision has proven difficult to enforce. For example, in 1974, the Supreme Court ruled that only deliberate attempts to gerrymander school districts in metropolitan regions in order to achieve segregation came under the 1954 ruling. Since urban-suburban segregation is so well institutionalized (by past *de jure* policies), this ruling is likely to forestall school integration within metropolitan regions. The irony is that *de jure* policies in one sector of the society (housing) have now become legally defined as a *de facto* situation in another sector (education)—a subtle form of legal discrimination that, coupled with legal inattention to the discrimination built into the internal structure of American schools themselves, will perpetuate the oppressive profile of American education.

Legal Discrimination in Politics

In the political arena, similar legal inattention to informal and formal practices of black disenfranchisement and exclusion can be found. In fact, only in the late 1950s and early 1960s was a significant legal attempt made to give blacks full-fledged political rights. The Voting Rights Acts of the 1960s were critical, because they made illegal many of the tactics, such as the poll tax, literacy test, and bureaucratic hassling, that had kept blacks unregistered and disenfranchised. Somewhat earlier, the Supreme Court in its famous "one man, one vote" ruling struck a blow against blatant gerrymandering of congressional districts along racial lines. But these laws and court decisions are fairly recent. Their impact has yet to be translated into full and proportionate representation, to say nothing of correcting for the consequences in other institutional spheres of black exclusion from the centers of power. If a minority is to redress its grievances and change oppressive structures, it must have a means for mobilizing power.

Summary

Through existing statutes and statutory omissions, law legitimates existing arrangements in a society. In the United States, a complex pattern of legitimated oppression has been evident. Until the last decades, laws have tended to be explicitly discriminatory in housing. In the political arena, state laws have been indirectly discriminatory by allowing differential enforcement of "universal" voter eligibility requirements for blacks and whites. By the failure to enact countervailing laws, the federal government sustained discrimination in voter registration and, hence, the political exclusion of blacks. In the job market, laws were racist by virtue of their absence in securing the Thirteenth and Fourteenth Amendment rights of black Americans. In education, legal uninvolvement allowed for local discriminatory laws and informal practices to prevail. In all institutional spheres, current congressional acts and Supreme Court decisions consistently encounter resistance as they seek to change prevailing institutional arrangements. Thus, past legal neglect and inattention to the rights of blacks, as well as direct legal discrimination, have helped create a profile of institutional arrangements that, even given the will, cannot now be easily legislated away.

There are several reasons for this impotency of current laws. First, institutional arrangements are not easily changed, because they embody the beliefs and habitual behaviors of the majority. Second, the laws are not always enforced because of meager enforcement resources. Third, the laws themselves do not always address the problem of past inequities, thrusting the burden of change on individual blacks who have now suddenly been given "equal opportunity." Current laws allow white Americans to reaffirm egalitarian values and at the same time to avoid significantly altering the structural arrangements that violate these values.

Oppression of Blacks by Agents
of Social Control

Throughout their history in the Americas and to the present day, blacks have encountered oppressive acts by agents of social control. Not only have these agents been involved in enforcing discriminatory laws, they have themselves often broken the law and engaged in coercive acts against blacks. The most frequent encounter of blacks with the police and courts has been over the issue of black resistance to formal laws and informal practices that deny them equality with whites.

Until the Civil War, it was against the law for most blacks to move about freely, to read and write, to choose a marriage partner, to own property, and to associate with whites or free blacks. This situation made it almost impossible for a black person to avoid violating some law. But often blacks deliberately fought against their oppression as codified in law.

Slave Revolts

The first record of a slave revolt in the New World dates back to 1526. As early as 1687, a slave insurrection took place in Virginia while whites congregated for a funeral. Early revolts were quickly put down by the dominant whites and, as a result, laws were passed recommending harsh punishments for such law violations. Dubois reports that during this period "crucifixion, burning and starvation were legal modes of punishment for slaves" (in Foster, 1959:38). From the early 1700s until the Civil War, there is evidence that slave revolts were common occurrences throughout the country. For example, in New York City there was a slave revolt in 1712. It was quickly put down, and twenty-one of the apprehended slaves were killed. One was hanged, another was publicly broken on "the wheel," and others were burned or mutilated and then hanged. A slave called "Cato" led a South Carolina slave revolt in 1739. The revolt lasted longer than most and spread to neighboring plantations. But Cato and his co-conspirators were eventually captured and punished much like their brethren in New York (Foster 1959:42). As these and the following examples illus-

trate, violations of discriminatory laws and/or informal practices have had the ironic consequence of encouraging the enactment of even more discriminatory laws and enforcement
policies.

By 1786, many northern whites were helping blacks break
the law. For example, it was in that year that George Washington was known to have complained about the Quakers'
organized efforts to liberate southern slaves and help fugitives
escape to the North. In 1804, with Quaker help, the Underground Railroad was publicly incorporated, and black leaders
like Harriet Tubman made a career of violating the law in order
to help their people rise above slavery (Franklin, 1974:198).

Practically every native American tribe in the southern
United States helped blacks violate the law by welcoming runaway slaves into their communities on a permanent basis. As
we indicated in chapter 4, in 1816 the federal government
lashed out against this form of law violation by attacking an
abandoned fort that had been claimed by local Indians and a
band of runaway blacks numbering over a thousand. These
early American "criminals" resisted valiantly, but after ten
days the "Negro Fort" was captured, and all blacks who remained alive were executed (Foster, 1959:100).

Around 1800 in Virginia, a massive slave revolt involving
thousands of blacks was discovered just moments before it
was scheduled to commence. In this case a house slave gave
the plot away. The startled whites quickly formed vigilante
groups and summoned troops. This resulted in approximately
35 blacks being put to death while no whites suffered injury.
Thereafter, federal troops were permanently stationed in Virginia. In 1811 another revolt broke out in New Orleans. It
involved several hundred black slaves. The revolt was immediately put down, and 65 blacks died in the aftermath.
Countless others perished while running from whites into the
woods (Foster, 1959:64).

Denmark Vesey is another notable law violator of the nineteenth century. In 1822, Vesey, a free black who had immi-
grated to South Carolina from the Caribbean, organized over
ten thousand slaves to revolt. When his plan was given away
by another house slave, Vesey's revolt was crushed. About
three dozen blacks were hanged and 43 more were banished

from South Carolina (Foster 1959:101).

In 1829 David Walker, a free black from Boston, drafted his famous pamphlet "Walker's Appeal" and sent thousands of bundled copies throughout the South. The pamphlet outlined the repressive state in which southern blacks lived and encouraged them to rise up and overthrow their masters through the use of violence. Although the pamphlets were gathered up by whites and destroyed, some southern slaves surely read Walker's words. In reaction, Virginia enacted in 1831 a law prohibiting blacks from preaching. Soon thereafter, the Maryland legislature outlawed assemblies of more than five blacks, even for purposes of worship. These initial reactions started a wave of even greater repression of blacks that swept throughout the southern states (Foster, 1959:98).

In 1831 Nat Turner, a slave, led another revolt in Virginia that was more successful and violent than most. Turner and his band of 70 or so armed slaves escaped from their plantation and terrorized whites in the Southampton area. Before they were captured, 61 whites had been killed and federal troops had to be called in order to put the revolt down. For joining with Turner, 120 slaves were immediately killed. Later 53 others were tried in court. Sixteen of them were hanged, while many others were imprisoned or otherwise punished (Foster, 1959:104).

This chain of events prompted most southern legislatures to restrict even further the movement of slaves and free blacks. They did this by enacting illegal assembly, curfew, and additional Jim Crow measures, making it even more difficult for blacks to avoid violating some law. For example, in 1838 black leader Frederick Douglass fled to the North, thus obtaining a criminal label. In fact, Foster (1959:41) reports that, like Douglass, thousands of slaves who did not openly revolt otherwise violated the law. "Slaves ran away, committed suicide, idled on the job, pretended illness, refused to bear children, burned plantations, and killed tyrannical overseers and planters."

Blacks and Northern Police

In the North, where before the Civil War blacks were already somewhat urbanized, the black arrest rate was much higher than that for whites. This is not surprising since many northern blacks were new arrivals to the city, often without means of support and guidance. Moreover, they lived in the decayed centers of northern American cities, where violence and vice traditionally abound. The higher arrest rate among blacks continued to escalate after the Civil War, as increased numbers of southern blacks moved to urban centers. Many blacks in the North were caught up in the violence of the labor movement. Other blacks, without property of their own, lashed out and stole in order to support themselves.

Other areas of employment that were open to poor urban blacks were gambling and prostitution. All these pursuits naturally brought blacks in conflict with the law. Those most susceptible to such temptations are the young, and as a result, each major American city, in the North and the South alike, soon developed major crime problems involving black youth. In this context most major northern municipal police departments were born. The first large, professional northern police organizations emerged towards the end of the Reconstruction period, ostensibly to combat labor and race riots as well as juvenile lawlessness.

It should be noted that this relationship between youthful crime and the creation of urban police organizations is not unique to the United States or to black Americans. For example, the first permanent police department in London had been created "to combat the hordes of unruly children who infest the streets." In this case, the "hordes of unruly children"were white and had left their farms in rural England and come to London with their poor, uneducated parents in pursuit of jobs and security that often did not exist. Urban crime and its relation to black youth is a serious problem indeed, but it is also an inevitable concomitant of rapid urbanization and industrialization.

Blacks and the Law in the South

In the South after the Civil War, arrest rates for blacks soared. Freed slaves who could not find jobs were jailed and then "contracted out," that is, they were sentenced by local courts to serve time on "chain gangs" and, in turn, contracted out to private entrepreneurs to work in agriculture, in railroad construction, or in other fields of commerce. This pattern of contracting brutalized thousands of blacks, while allowing whites to realize great profit from the labor of blacks (as had slave traders and owners). And once its profitability was recognized, this and other similar practices made the southern black an especially attractive target of the law.

It was also during this time that the lynching of blacks reached its zenith. Many blacks were lynched after being convicted by local courts for the rape or murder of a white person. Hundreds of other black southerners were lynched, or sometimes tortured and burned as an alternative, because a black was rumored to have raped or murdered a white. In these times of southern panic and malevolent action, there was little concern with guaranteeing due legal process before getting on with the punishment. Throughout the South, all that was necessary was a fearful crowd, whispers of murder or rape of a white woman, and an unfortunate black who happened to get caught walking in the wrong part of town. With a rope and a tree, or some flammable materials, blacks could be punished and kept in line with a minimum of legal red tape. Because these practices were efficient enforcement techniques, and because there was no loud clamor from a powerful constituency to do otherwise, it seems that local southern law enforcement officers and local courts adopted a policy of "benign neglect" towards enforcing the civil rights of blacks who were caught in such circumstances.

Recent Arrest Rates

Over the last five decades, from 1930 to the present, we can get an indirect glimpse at relations between police and blacks by examining arrest rates of blacks. Statistics such as these do not tell us about informal, nonarrest relations between police and blacks, but they give us a comparative sense of how often the police and blacks formally confront one another. From the FBI's efforts to compile data on crimes, it is now possible to make several generalizations. These data reveal many methodological problems, but they are considerably better than dis-

cursive historical accounts. Recognizing that there are methodological problems involved, the FBI's Uniform Crime
Reports (1980) reveal that:
1. For most criminal offenses, the arrest rate for blacks is
    three times that of whites.
2. Although blacks comprise only 12 percent of the popu-
    lation, they continue to account for approximately 50
    percent of all arrests for murder, rape, robbery, assault,
    weapons offenses, and sex offenses other than rape.
3. The vast majority of blacks are arrested for minor of-
    fenses, however. These include drug use, alcohol, and
    petty stealing.
4. Most crimes for which blacks are arrested are committed
    by teenagers.

It is impossible to know, of course, if such an arrest record
reflects higher crime rates among blacks or prejudicial enforcement of the law. It is clear that the poor commit more common
crimes than the affluent, and that blacks are, on the average,
poor. But is their crime rate greater than would be expected
from other categories of poor? Clear answers to such a question
are not currently available. But once arrested, blacks no longer
seem to suffer great discrimination as they once did in local
courts. Table 6.1 documents the average sentences for nonwhites (who are mostly blacks) and whites for various types
of crime. The table shows that blacks continue to serve more
time than do whites for some comparable offenses, but there
are some offenses for which the opposite is also true. Trial
judges and lawyers explain that blacks spend more time in jail
and prison because they more often have been convicted of
prior crimes and, thus, deserve more harsh treatment. If blacks
are more "criminal" than whites, it is very likely due to where
they live and what they are forced to do for a living.

Despite their encounters with the police and courts, blacks
still appear to place considerable trust in agents of social control. For example, public opinion surveys reported by Hindelang (1977) show that as many blacks as whites say the
police are doing a "good" or "average" job; three of four blacks
say that the police should be "tougher" in dealing with crime

TABLE 6.1.

Average sentences for convicted persons committed to federal prisons by offense and race, 1979.

Offense	Average sentence (in months)	
	Nonwhites	Whites
Kidnapping[1]	218.5	187.0
Robbery[1]	135.4	134.1
Assault[1,2]	57.3	39.1
Drug laws[1,2]	56.0	48.9
Burglary	40.3	51.9
Extortion	70.5	75.4
White-slave traffic	42.0	60.5
Securities violations	27.0	46.3
Forgery	30.4	37.1
Larceny[2]	29.8	37.4
Counterfeiting	33.7	37.6
Firearms violations	32.6	34.5
Fraud	23.3	27.5
Income tax violations[1,2]	25.3	14.7
Liquor law violations	24.8	15.6
Immigration law violations[1]	9.0	5.5

[1] Offenses for which nonwhites receive longer average sentences than whites.
[2] Offenses where gross discrepancies in sentencing exist.

Source: U.S. Department of Justice, Federal Bureau of Prisons (1979), p. 488.

and lawlessness; and more blacks than whites, when asked, say that they have "respect" and "confidence" in the Supreme Court.

Legal Oppression: An Overview

If oppressive social arrangements are to endure, they must be legitimated and enforced. Legitimation comes from cultural beliefs and legal statutes. Enforcement comes from the police, courts, and prisons. In this chapter, we have sought to document briefly that the legal system in America—that is, law-enacting bodies, law-enforcing agencies, and law-adjudicating structures such as the courts—has historically operated to legitimate the oppression of black Americans. It has done so in several ways. First, the legal system has codified into law highly discriminatory practices, and in so doing, bestowed legitimacy on racist beliefs. Second, the legal system has not outlawed many discriminatory acts until after the damage to black opportunities has already been done. Third, the legal system has often declared a discriminatory practice illegal but has not taken steps to correct for the past consequences of this practice. Fourth, the legal system has often not enforced existing antidiscriminatory laws. Fifth, until the last few decades, blacks have suffered severe discrimination by local courts and the police.

Thus, the legal system has been intimately involved in the oppression of blacks. While the courts in recent years have worked to reduce racial discrimination, it is difficult to legislate away beliefs and informal practices. This, coupled with the fact that the legacy of past discrimination has not been undone, means that racial oppression persists in America. In many ways, this is the new "American Dilemma": how to "correct" for past oppression without discrimination against affluent and powerful whites. Without enactment of both anti-discriminatory laws and compensatory measures (to undo the legacy of past discrimination), blacks will have great difficulty in reducing their oppression.

CHAPTER SEVEN

The Sociocultural
Dynamics of Oppression

In this last chapter, we will use our descriptive account of black-white relations in America to develop some tentative generalizations about the nature of racial and ethnic oppression. While white oppression of blacks in America represents an extreme case, the oppression of minorities by the majority is a long standing and pervasive property of social systems.

In this theoretical chapter, we will examine the more generic social dynamics of racial oppression. Our goal will be to understand (1) the social structural processes of oppression, (2) the cultural processes that accompany any enduring social pattern, and (3) the interrelationship between structural patterns, on the one hand, and cultural values and beliefs on the other. In this way, we can bring together into a more unified theoretical framework the descriptive materials presented in earlier chapters.

Theoretical Assumptions

The data presented in the previous chapters have been developed with few a priori assumptions. We have tried to "let the facts speak for themselves," yet when we seek to explain these facts, we must begin to invoke assumptions. No effort at theoretical explanation is purely inductive, and hence our efforts are not wholly inductive. On the contrary, we are proceeding with knowledge of existing theoretical efforts, from which we have drawn two assumptions:

1. All enduring patterns of social relationship among populations in a society are directly related to diverse economic interests in a society.
2. All enduring patterns of social relationship persist because those interests with the most power can codify a system of beliefs to legitimate such patterns.

In following this first assumption, we have been led to Bonacich's (1972) "theory of the split labor market." This theory, we feel, does a better job than others[1] in capturing the basic structural dynamics of "ethnic antagonisms." In general, the split labor market theory translates racial and ethnic social patterns into class antagonisms. The theory views such antagonisms as resulting from the divided interests of three parties: (1) capitalists, or those who employ labor to produce goods and services for a profit; (2) higher-priced labor, who depend upon capitalists for the maintenance of wages and their standard of living; and (3) low-priced workers, who are willing and able to perform the same work as higher-priced labor for less money. Capitalists are seen as having an interest in increasing profits by reducing labor costs. Higher-priced workers are viewed as having an interest in maintaining and raising their wages in the face of all "threats" by capitalists or other workers. Lower-priced labor is seen as having an interest in working, per se, even for wages that are lower than those traditionally paid. In such a situation, capitalists have an interest in hiring lower-priced workers. This threatens higher-priced workers in ways that increase efforts to keep lower-priced workers out of the higher-priced labor market. The dynamics of race and ethnic relations, Bonacich argues, ultimately boil down to these basic forces.[2]

Oppression of a minority typically stems from the fact that the minority, for variable reasons, finds itself in a position of having to offer its labor for less if it is to work. As a result, capitalists will use the labor of the minority for as little compensation as is necessary to induce work. Higher-priced labor will seek to exclude the minority from the labor market or, if exclusion is not possible, to keep the minority partitioned in a limited range of economic roles that do not threaten to undercut their income. Under these conditions, oppression of the minority comes from two sources: (1) capitalists, who want to exploit minority labor dependent on them for work, and (2) higher-priced workers who want to keep minority labor from undercutting their standard of living.

Many of the dynamics of black-white relations in America can be understood in these terms. Yet, in Bonacich's theory, as well as other structural arguments (Blauner, 1972; Noel, 1968; van den Berghe, 1967; Schermerhorn, 1970; Lieberson, 1961; W.J. Wilson, 1973), cultural processes are too often seen as "residual" or as mere ideological justifications for exploitation. There is little doubt that exploiters develop beliefs to legitimate their activities, as the discussion in previous chapters underscores. But we will argue that cultural values and beliefs have more direct consequences for alterations in patterns of oppression than structural theorists like Bonacich typically acknowledge. Conflicts and contradictions between values and beliefs often provide a major impetus to change, not just in cultural symbols but also in social structural arrangements. These considerations follow from our second assumption and will guide our efforts to modify the split labor market theory.

The Data Consolidated

In the previous chapters, we have described the structure and culture of white oppression of blacks in America from the seventeenth century to the present. In order to use these "data" to develop a theory, as well as to confirm our operating assumptions, we need to consolidate the information presented in previous chapters. Table 7.1 extracts data from earlier chapters and presents this information in highly abbreviated form. This table is included for convenience and for the purpose of checking to see if the generalizations to follow "fit" with the historical record.[3]

TABLE 7.1.

A summary of the structure of racial oppression and racial beliefs in American history.

Period[a]	Structure of Oppression[b]	Dominant Beliefs[c]	"Progressive" Beliefs[c]
English Heritage –1650	1. Colonial expansion 2. Indentured servant system	1. Blacks are uncivilized heathens (19:ch. 1) 2. Blackness is evil—a curse of God (19:ch. 1) 3. Blacks are bestial by nature (19:ch. 1)	
Colonial America 1650–1760	1. Slave trade 2. Institutionalization of slavery	1. Black bestiality, especially their sexual aggressiveness, requires control (19:ch. 3)	
Revolutionary Era 1760–1820	1. Abolition of slave trade 2. Confinement of slavery to the South	1. Slavery is a "necessary evil" (19:ch. 7) 2. Blacks are ill-suited or unprepared for freedom (19:ch. 7)	1. Slavery is inconsistent with revolutionary ideology (19:ch. 7) 2. While culturally deprived and debased by slavery, blacks are capable of betterment (19:ch. 7)

170

Table 7.1. (continued)

Period[a]	Structure of Oppression[b]	Dominant Beliefs[c]	"Progressive" Beliefs[c]
Antebellum Era 1820–1860	1. Further institutionalization of slavery in the face of ideological challenges and North-South economic and political competition 2. Spread of northern Jim Crow practices	1. Slavery is a "positive good" that protects the interests of masters and slaves alike (10:ch. 2; 17; 35) 2. Slavery harnesses the savage nature of blacks, civilizing them as far as possible (10:ch. 2; 17; 35) 3. The childlike dependency of blacks requires white protection (10:ch. 2; 17; 35) 4. Northern stereotype defines blacks as ignorant, lazy, and immoral (23; 35)	1. There are "racial" differences (10:ch. 4) 2. Blacks' "childlike simplicity" reveals a basic Christian nature (10:ch. 4) 3. Slavery is morally wrong—it corrupts and takes advantage of a naturally submissive people (10:ch. 4)

Table 7.1. (continued)

Period[a]	Structure of Oppression[b]	Dominant Beliefs[c]	"Progressive" Beliefs[c]
Civil War and Reconstruction 1861–1877			
Postreconstruction to WWI 1877–1914	1. Dismantling of Radical Reconstruction 2. Growing legalized segregation in all institutional spheres 3. Relegation of blacks to menial farm-factory occupations 4. Enforcement of segregation and relegation through white violence 5. Legalized and de facto disenfranchisement	1. Black corruption in Reconstruction confirms their inherent inferiority (13:ch. 11; 21) 2. Blacks have failed to take advantage of "equal" opportunities and, in accordance with Social Darwinism, should be left to find their social niche (10:pp. 175–86 and ch. 8; 13:ch. 7) 3. Without the supervision and compulsion of slavery, blacks have degenerated to their natural state, where they are lazy, prone to crime, and lust for white women (10:ch. 9; 18)	1. The Negro race is less advanced than the white because it has not progressed as far on the scale of evolution (10:ch. 10; 15) 2. Blacks are potentially useful citizens—their natural docility and kindness can be channeled through education, industrial training, and white guidance (10:ch. 10) 3. Racial purity and the instinct of race prejudice necessitate racial segregation (10:ch. 10)

Table 7.1. (continued)

Period[a]	Structure of Oppression[b]	Dominant Beliefs[c]	"Progressive" Beliefs[c]
		4. The traits of blacks that make them different from and inferior to whites require separation of the races (10:ch. 9; 18)	
WWI to WWII 1914–1941	1. Northern migration of southern blacks and their confinement to ghettos	1. Black inferiority is an indisputable scientific fact, backed by evolutionary theory and intelligence testing (13:chs. 14 and 15; 26)	1. All apparent social, cultural, and intellectual differences between the races are the result of the environment (13:ch. 16; 24:ch. 4)
	2. Last hired and first fired policy	2. Segregationist doctrine continues to be affirmed: racial segregation is natural and instinctive, for the good of and desired by both races; blacks are permanently inferior beings necessitating segregation to control their criminality and lust and to guard against amalgamation (13:ch. 11; 24:ch. 4; 26)	2. Blacks are the victims of an oppressive environment that creates discontent, frustration, and a fatalistic sense of powerlessness (13:ch. 16; 24:ch. 4)
	3. Union exclusion and confinement to low-scaled occupations		
	4. Segregation and disenfranchisement backed by violence, formal law, and de facto practices		

173

Table 7.1. (continued)

Period[a]	Structure of Oppression[b]	Dominant Beliefs[c]	"Progressive" Beliefs[c]
WWII through Second Reconstruction 1941–1968	1. Efforts to increase opportunity without alterations of basic institutional and community patterns 2. Efforts to keep domestic tranquility through control by welfare system 3. Community and economic resistance to integration 4. Sporadic and inconsistent government pressure to decrease segregation and exclusion	1. Rejection of legal segregation (16; 34; 14) 2. Blacks have been discriminated against in the past (2:ch. 6; 33:ch. 4; 7) 3. Blacks are not inherently inferior to whites and are capable of change (34:20; 32) 4. Change is best accomplished by improving substandard schools, and renovating black ghettos, providing more vocational schools, and renovating black ghettos, in other words, by providing "equal opportunities" (34:chs. 3 and 4; 11:1961)	1. Black appearances of inferiority reflect cultural deprivation and the impact of undesirable environments (28:6) 2. Complete social integration is the only viable means to racial harmony (31; 36; 28; 30) 3. Forced integration of schools is essential to any program of change (3; 29)

174

Table 7.1. (continued)

Period[a]	Structure of Oppression[b]	Dominant Beliefs[c]	"Progressive" Beliefs[c]
1968–present	1. Continued de facto residential segregation 2. White violence and protest of educational integration 3. Decreased political and legal efforts to enforce civil rights legislation, even in the face of "affirmative action" policies	1. Blacks' inferior status is largely attributable to blacks themselves, especially their lack of motivation (9; 32; 4) 2. The pace of change in race relations has been too fast (8; 27:44–45) 3. Enough has been done—reverse discrimination and forced integration measures such as open housing laws and busing are wrong (27:45; 22; 5; 12)	1. Racism is generic to the social structure of American society (25; 7) 2. The "equal opportunities" doctrine has failed—there is need to redress for past wrongs (1:ch. 8; 20:ch. 6) 3. Immediate integration is not possible—community control and group power are more practicable (1; 20:chs. 7 and 8)

Table 7.1. (continued)

ᵃ Dates correspond to the following historical events:

1650: roughly marks the beginning of the distinction, soon recognized in law, between indentured servitude for whites and lifetime servitude for blacks

1760: first serious antislavery crusade gets into full swing (see Jordan, 1968:ch. 7)

1820: height of debates leading to the Missouri Compromise; re-emergence of strong antislavery sentiment

1860: election of Lincoln; beginning of southern secession

1877: election of Hayes; withdrawal of federal troops from the South

1914: World War I

1941: World War II

1948: Truman establishes Commission on Civil Rights, issues executive order desegregating armed forces

1968: assassination of Martin Luther King; publication of the Kerner Report; election of Nixon

ᵇ The structure of racial oppression in America is well documented. A useful chronology of major events in black history is contained in Polski and Kaiser (1971:1–27). Also see Franklin (1961) and Frazier (1957).

References: 1. Blauner (1972). 2. Brink and Harris (1966). 3. Brown v. Board of Education (1954). 4. Angus Campbell (1971). 5. Current Opinion (1975). 6. Deutsch, Katz, and Jensen (1968). 7. Erskine (1968a). 8. Erskine (1968b). 9. Erskine (1968c). 10. Fredrickson (1971). 11. Gallup (1972). 12. Gallup Opinion Index (1975). 13. Gossett (1963). 14. Greeley and Sheatsley (1971). 15. Haller (1971). 16. Hyman and Sheatsley (1964). 17. Jenkins (1935). 18. Guion Johnson (1949). 19. Jordan (1968). 20. Killian (1975). 21. Kincaid (1970). 22. Levine (1971–1972). 23. Litwack (1961). 24. Myrdal (1944). 25. NAACD (1968). 26. Newby (1965). 27. Newsweek (1969). 28. Pettigrew (1964). 29. Pettigrew (1969a). 30. Pettigrew (1969b). 31. Raab and Lipset (1962). 32. Schuman (1969). 33. Schwartz (1967). 34. Sheatsley (1966). 35. Takaki (1970). 36. R. M. Williams (1964).

We have already examined the general trends evident in the structure and culture of oppression, yet we should briefly review some of these trends, since they "confirm" some of our operating assumptions and suggest how these assumptions can be translated into more explicit propositions.

In the column on the left are eight historical periods that mark distinctive patterns in the structure of oppression. In the middle column are delineated the dominant beliefs of each epoch. And in the right column are summarized beliefs that we term "progressive." This distinction represents the major kind of variation in beliefs that we found in any given period. On the one hand were a set of "dominant" beliefs, held by a majority of the population, that were consistent with the actual structure of oppression. On the other hand were a set of "progressive" beliefs, with a wide minority following, that challenged both dominant beliefs and the structure of oppression in varying degrees. For example, as we noted in chapter 2, the proslavery doctrine was opposed by the abolitionist position during the antebellum period.

By reading down and across the columns, several trends are evident in this profile of structural arrangements, dominant beliefs, and progressive beliefs. These can be summarized as follows:

1. Dominant beliefs legitimate the structure of oppression for each period.
2. These dominant beliefs have changed over time from those emphasizing biological factors as "explanations" for the subordinate position of blacks to those stressing "psycho-cultural" factors.
3. Alterations in dominant beliefs appear to correspond to alterations in the structural form of black oppression.
4. Progressive beliefs have shifted from those that stress racial differences—whether biological or cultural—to those that highlight the oppressiveness of American social structure.
5. At certain times there has been considerable conflict between dominant and progressive beliefs; at other times such conflict is less severe.

6. Progressive beliefs, at times, challenge the structure of oppression.
7. Changes in the structure of oppression appear most likely to occur during, or immediately after, those periods when conflict between dominant and progressive beliefs is greatest and when progressive beliefs severely challenge the structure of oppression.
8. Changes in the structure of oppression are not as extensive as those stipulated by progressive beliefs.

These conclusions are far from definitive. Many unique and idiosyncratic historical events have had a profound influence on beliefs and social structural arrangements. For example, four full-scale war mobilizations, industrialization, urbanization, and demographic changes in the age, sex, and race structure, as well as in mobility, have all operated to alter the structure and culture of oppression. Yet, despite these events, there still appears to be considerable patterning in beliefs as well as between beliefs and the structure of oppression. A theory cannot explain the idiosyncratic, only those events that reveal a pattern. Our theoretical efforts must concentrate on developing a theory that can explain these patterns or trends.

The Theory[4]

Scope Conditions

Any theory must begin with a statement of scope conditions. No theory can explain everything; hence we need to specify those historical conditions in American society that limit the scope of the theory. Our theory of oppression can be applied only to those social systems that reveal the following attributes:
1. a market system for the distribution of labor, or at least some portion of the labor force;
2. a population that—in terms of cultural, social, or biological features—can be divided into distinctive and identifiable subpopulations;
3. an economic system in which, for a variety of historical reasons, distinctive populations occupy different economic positions that reveal varying levels of remuneration;

4. a cultural system in which values emphasizing individual freedom and liberty as well as social equality are prominent components; and

5. a political system in which societal members can legitimately exert political pressures on decisionmakers.[5]

These conditions are limiting, but they exist in many societies. Hence, the theory that is proposed has wide applicability, particularly in Western societies that have experienced industrialization and the immigration of culturally (and biologically) distinctive populations. For example, the United States, most societies in western Europe, Australia, New Zealand, South Africa, and several other African nations meet these conditions.

Theoretical Propositions

The data presented in earlier chapters and summarized in abbreviated form in table 7.1 can be interpreted in terms of nine theoretical propositions. The first two propositions represent a revised statement of Bonacich's split labor market theory and may be stated as follows:

1. The higher the wages of the work force in a society, the greater will be its perceived threat in the face of market penetration by a low-wage labor pool, especially if:
   a. the low-wage labor pool is identifiable in terms of biological or cultural characteristics.
   b. the potential employers (capitalists) of labor have incentives to hire low-wage labor.
   c. the low-wage labor cannot be excluded from the labor market.
2. The less its ability to exclude a low-wage labor pool from the labor market, the more likely is the higher-wage and threatened work force to seek policies creating a caste system of occupations, especially if:
   a. low-wage labor has entered the labor market at an initial competitive disadvantage.
   b. the higher-wage and threatened work force has political-economic organization and resources.

    c. potential employers of low-wage labor are econom-
       ically dependent upon the loyalty and services of
       the threatened, higher-wage work force.

These two propositions indicate the conditions under which higher-wage labor becomes threatened by a population that could potentially undercut wages by virtue of its willingness to perform the same work for less money. Such threat is heightened when low-wage labor is readily identified (proposition 1a), when employers have incentives for hiring low-wage labor (1b), and when the low-wage labor cannot be excluded from the labor market (1c). Such threat can become translated into economic and political pressures by higher-wage labor to confine cheap labor to only a limited range of low-paying economic roles, thereby creating a caste system. These efforts are likely to be most effective when cheap labor is at an initial disadvantage in terms of skill levels, political influence, and tradition of high-wage labor (2a), when the more expensive labor force has viable economic and political organizations such as labor unions and political parties (2b), and when potential employers of cheap labor are not able to ignore completely the demands of higher-wage labor (2c).

Many of the changing patterns of structured oppression of blacks over America's history represent the efforts of the majority work force to confine blacks in certain low-paying occupations that do not threaten higher-wage labor. From one viewpoint, the Civil War itself represents a more macro-application of the processes contained in these propositions. As the South began to industrialize and compete with the industrial North, it had a large, low-wage labor pool (slaves) that could keep southern capitalists' costs low and enable them to threaten northern industrialists (Bonacich, 1975). Subsequent to the Civil War, segregationist practices, relegation to menial farm occupations, "last hired and first fired policies," housing discrimination, and ghettoization can be viewed as successive efforts to perpetuate the caste position of blacks and thus avoid the consequences of their free movement in the labor market. Such practices were, no doubt, intensified as employers sought to use blacks as strikebreakers. For example, as we noted in earlier chapters, Bonacich (1976) documented the rates of interracial violence during the early decades of this century as a reaction of whites to the efforts of capitalists to use blacks as strikebreakers to undermine the union movement. Such acts of white violence and black retaliation escalated hostilities and the negative perceptions of whites and blacks toward each other.

Caste Beliefs. Whether more peaceful or violent means are employed to keep cheap labor "in its place," the result is for the majority and higher-wage labor force to develop beliefs that legitimate their oppressive efforts. Thus, we need to introduce a third proposition:

3. The greater the efforts of the threatened and higher-wage work force to seek and perpetuate a caste system, the more likely are they to hold discriminatory beliefs legitimating the caste system,[6] especially if:
    a. a caste system violates the core values of the society.
    b. a caste system violates the beliefs of other segments of the non-caste population.
    c. the identifiable groups subject to the caste system represent a potential, or actual, political force in their own right.
    d. the potential employers of low-wage labor have an economic incentive to keep wages low.

Caste systems are most effective when those in lower ranks are defined as "inferior." As more expensive labor initiates pressures for the creation of a caste, beliefs tend to stress the "inferior" character of cheap labor. If the low-wage labor can be identified biologically, then their inferiority can be seen as a biological fact. The negative stereotypes of blacks as "bestial," "childlike," "immoral," "lazy," and "less intelligent" have all been used to justify the caste position of blacks in American society. The equivalent of these negative stereotypes can be found in other societies where caste relations are evident.

In American society and in Western societies in general, caste relations contradict basic values of equality and freedom. The existence of castes contradicts other basic values, posing, as Myrdal (1944) emphasized, an "American Dilemma." For

example, borrowing from Robin M. Williams' (1970) typology
of basic values, caste social relations violate the core values
of "activism," "achievement," "individualism," and "equality."[7] In order to reduce the contradictions between caste and
these core values, it becomes necessary to construct beliefs
that view subordinated minorities as either innately inferior,
and hence, not fully covered by these values, or as not meeting
these values because of flaws in their character, and hence,
not worthy of positions outside of their caste.

Typically, as beliefs in innate inferiority become less tena-
ble, beliefs about the "character" of the subjugated are used
to legitimate their oppression. Thus, over the course of American history, the "rights" of blacks to be "active," to "achieve,"
to be "individuals," and to be "equal" were not violated as
long as blacks could be considered inferior and "less than
equal." From early Elizabethan notions of bestial black heath-
ens, through conceptions of blacks as ignorant, lazy, and immoral savages, to late nineteenth-century notions of blacks as
having degenerated to their natural state, and to more recent
conceptions of blacks as culturally impoverished and as un-
motivated, each epoch in American history has witnessed the
majority of the population—that is, the threatened work
force—holding beliefs that have legitimated different structures of oppression, while at the same time resolving conflicts
between core values and these patterns of oppression.

Such beliefs are also used to galvanize resistance to political
resistance by the oppressed (proposition 3c above) and by
other segments of the population who adhere to the core values
and who see the contradictions between racist beliefs and core
values (3b). Moreover, racist beliefs can also serve to mobilize
sentiment against employers who might seek to undercut
wages by hiring "inferior" workers (3d).

Progressive Beliefs. As is evident from table 7.1, dominant
beliefs are often challenged by more progressive beliefs that
emphasize the contradictions between a caste system and its
legitimating beliefs, on the one hand, and a society's core values of equality and freedom, on the other. Such beliefs are
most likely to be held by those who are not threatened by the
penetration of low-wage labor into the market. For example,

Donald (1956:27-31) notes that abolitionists were unthreatened by black market penetration, for they tended to come
from the professional groups of doctors, lawyers, priests, and
successful commercial business people. Moreover, as Donald
(1956:31) stresses, abolitionists were "not so much hostile to
labor as indifferent to it . . . [since] the factory worker represented an alien and unfamiliar system toward which the antislavery leaders felt no kinship or responsibility." Thus, abolitionists perceived no threat from emancipation and the
market penetration of blacks, and it was for this reason that
they were the most likely to codify challenging beliefs.

Another group frequently codifying challenging beliefs are
academics, such as Franz Boas, who led the ideological attack
on racism in the 1920s and 1930s. However, in recent years,
academics have been less vocal as "affirmative action" policies
in a tight job market have seriously threatened, for the first
time in history, their economic position. These considerations
lead us to formulate two additional propositions:

4. The less a population is threatened by a low-wage labor
   pool, the less likely is it to view castes as desirable or
   necessary, especially if:
   a. they are detached from extensive relations with the
      threatened work force.
   b. they are detached from those economic positions
      that would be influenced by an influx of low-wage
      labor.
5. The more a population is segregated from the threatened
   work force and from relevant economic positions, the
   more likely is it to view the contradictions between caste
   processes and legitimating beliefs on the one hand and
   the core values of the society on the other,[8] especially if:
   a. core values stress individual freedom and egalitar-
      ianism.
   b. beliefs are explicitly discriminatory and in violation
      of core values.

In asking who is likely to hold progressive beliefs, we also
discovered that political elites are often among those holding
such beliefs. In America, this is particularly likely since the
political system is not typified by strong party organization

regulating the selection of elites and since the system encourages political elites to be "their own person." Political elites in America have often been detached from the higher-wage constituency that is threatened by the removal of caste barriers. In fact, political decision-makers and their advisors are often drawn from unthreatened professions, such as law. These elites and their advisors have been, we contend, more likely to see the "American Dilemma," and because they are strategically placed to initiate changes in the pattern of oppression, they often do. Such change is usually initiated after a period of ideological codification of beliefs that challenge the dominant racist beliefs and the oppressive structures these beliefs legitimate.

Such codification of challenging beliefs provides political elites with legitimation from core values to initiate changes. For example, the conflict between dominant and progressive beliefs during and after the Revolutionary War, and the political debates this conflict generated, resulted in the abolition of the slave trade and in the abolition of slavery in the North. To take perhaps the most obvious example, the ideological attacks of abolitionists on the evils of slavery helped initiate the Civil War and provided justification to elites for emancipation (see McPherson, 1964). Changes in the pattern of discrimination in housing, schools, and unions in the post-World War II period came after considerable codification of social science beliefs about cultural deprivation and of the need to provide "equal opportunities." However, as is revealed by the long period between the end of Radical Reconstruction and the start of World War II, little change in structural arrangements is likely to occur when progressive beliefs do not directly challenge dominant beliefs and the structured oppression they legitimate. Up until World War I, progressive beliefs were simply more benign forms of dominant beliefs. In the post-World War I period, beliefs gradually became more progressive and began to challenge dominant beliefs, but other factors, such as the Depression and World War II, mitigated the impact of these beliefs on political elites until after World War II. These considerations lead us to formulate an additional proposition:

6. The greater the size of the detached population and the greater its political resources, the more likely is it to exert political pressures for mitigating the caste system, especially if:
    a. the political system encourages the incumbency of detached elites.
    b. the political system does not reveal strong party organization.
    c. segments of the detached population can codify a challenging system of beliefs exposing the contradictions between caste beliefs and core values.
    d. a media system allowing for the dissemination of the challenging beliefs is available.

Changing Beliefs and Structures. In table 7.1, we noted that structural changes have never corresponded fully to the tenets of challenging beliefs. The reason for this incomplete transformation of racist arrangements is that, as changes occur, the level of threat experienced by the higher-wage work force increases, and they then begin to use their political resources—union organization and large blocs of votes, for example—to resist political initiatives for change. In response to the perceived threat posed by incipient alterations of blacks' caste position, modified beliefs are codified to legitimate the new pattern of oppression. For example, the "positive good" theory of slavery in the antebellum South represented a reaffirmation of slavery in response to the challenge posed by abolitionists' ideological codification. More recently, the emphasis of present dominant beliefs on the "lack of motivation" among blacks and on "reverse discrimination" are being used to justify efforts at slowing governmental initiatives that threaten not just the position of higher wage labor but also the "whites only" lifestyle. These processes require that two additional propositions be added to the theory:

7. The more elites of the detached population can initiate structural changes in the caste position of the identifiable low-wage labor pool, the more threatened the higher-wage work force and the more organized politically they are likely to become, especially if:

    a. they represent a large proportion of the total work
       force in a society.

    b. changes in the caste position of a low-wage labor
       pool pose direct threats to wage levels of the higher-
       wage work force.

8. The more the higher-wage work force becomes politically
    organized, the greater its political power, the greater its
    capacity to limit alteration in the caste system, and the
    more likely is it to re-adjust beliefs legitimating the al-
    tered caste system.

Finally, with codification of a new set of racist beliefs and
their use to legitimate an altered structure of oppression, "progressive" beliefs eventually come to challenge dominant racist
beliefs and the oppression that they legitimate. As table 7.1
states, slavery as well as the belief in slavery as a "necessary
evil" were soon challenged by abolitionist beliefs. Over a long
period of American history, Jim Crow and other segregationist
practices, as well as the beliefs legitimating these practices,
were eventually challenged by progressive beliefs in the 1920s,
1930s, and 1940s. Presently, the belief that blacks "lack motivation," that "change is occurring too fast," and that discrimination is now "against whites" have yet to become sufficiently enduring to allow a challenging set of beliefs to be
codified by unthreatened segments of the population. Tenets
of present progressive beliefs that "America is racist" pose
little challenge to dominant beliefs because they do not indicate a concrete direction of change for detached political
elites. With the concrete threat posed by affirmative action in
a tightening academic job market, a traditional population for
belief codification may become sufficently threatened as to
limit the challenge of progressive beliefs. In the long run, it is
likely that challenging beliefs will be codified by unthreatened
segments of the population, thus necessitating the final proposition of the theory:

9. The more prolonged altered caste relations and legiti-
    mating beliefs, the more likely are detached segments of
    the population to initiate new political pressures and to
    codify revised challenging beliefs, in an effort to mitigate
    the perceived inconsistency between core values and the
    existence of a legitimated caste system.

These nine propositions, we believe, fit best with the data presented in earlier chapters and in table 7.1. As we have suggested, however, this theory can hopefully account for more than black-white relations in America. Much like Bonacich's split labor market theory, our revision can be extended to account for sociocultural processes that are likely to occur in societies that meet the scope conditions outlined earlier. Although our focus has been on American society, the theory can probably be generalized to other capitalist societies experiencing influxes of "ethnic labor" or "ethnic business entrepreneurs" willing to perform the same work for less. For example, the influx of Pakistani and Ugandan Asians into England has created both a split labor market and a split petty bourgeoisie, resulting in the codification of racist beliefs. Ethnic relations in England might well be a fertile arena for testing some of the implications of the theory.

The Theory Extended

One way to visualize the broader implications of the theory is to raise its level of abstraction. In so doing, the propositions may have even broader applicability not only to diverse forms of ethnic antagonism, but also to intergroup conflict in general. If we raise the level of abstraction in the theory, the following propositions emerge:

1. The greater the economic and social resources of groupings in a system, the more likely are these groupings to perceive threat in the face of another group's capacity to compete for shares of their resources, especially if:
   a. the threatening group is identifiable in terms of biological or cultural characteristics.
   b. other groupings in the system have an interest in supporting the efforts of the threatening group.
   c. the threatening group cannot be excluded from the system.
2. The less the capacity to exclude a threatening group, the more likely are threatened groupings to seek policies of internal exclusion from positions that allow them to compete for resources, especially if:
   a. the threatening group is initially at a disadvantage in its competition with the threatened groupings.

    b. the threatened groupings have political resources.

    c. nonthreatened sectors of the system are dependent upon the activities of the threatened groupings.

3. The greater the efforts of the threatened to internally exclude groups from positions that allow them to compete for resources, the more likely are the threatened to codify discriminating beliefs legitimating intrasystem exclusion, especially if:

    a. intrasystem exclusion contradicts core values and must therefore be reconciled with these core values.

    b. intrasystem exclusion contradicts beliefs of other, non-threatened groupings.

    c. excluded groups have, or could potentially acquire, political resources.

    d. other, non-threatened groupings have incentives to encourage resource competition.

4. The less threatened a grouping by resource competition from identifiable groupings, the less likely they are to support inter- or intrasystem exclusion practices especially if:

    a. they are detached from relations with threatened groupings.

    b. they are detached from positions around which the resource competition occurs.

5. The more detached a grouping, the more likely they are to view contradictions between exclusion practices and legitimating beliefs on the one hand and core values on the other, especially if:

    a. core values stress freedom and equality.

    b. beliefs legitimating exclusion are explicitly in violation of core values.

6. The greater the size and political resources of detached groupings, the more likely they are to exert political pressure for mitigating exclusion practices, especially if:

    a. the political system encourages incumbency of detached elites.

    b. the political system does not reveal strong party organization.

    c. some detached groupings can codify challenging beliefs.

    d. media are available for dissemination of challenging beliefs.

7. The more elites of detached groupings can initiate changes mitigating exclusion and increasing resource competition, the more threatened those groups facing the competition, and the more they are likely to become politically organized, especially if:
    a. threatened groups constitute a large proportion of a system's population.
    b. mitigation of exclusion practices creates direct and increased competition for resources.
8. The more threatened groups become politically organized, the greater their power, the greater their capacity to limit alterations of intrasystem exclusion, and the more likely they are to re-adjust and codify beliefs legitimating altered exclusion practices.
9. The more prolonged altered exclusion practices, the more likely are detached groupings to initiate new political pressures and to codify revised challenging beliefs in an effort to mitigate the perceived inconsistency between core values and legitimated exclusion practices.

By shifting the level of abstraction in this way, the theory can be used to explain competition for other than economic resources, and it can perhaps be used to describe caste processes in other than societal systems. For example, forced school busing has created political resistance and the codification of legitimating and racist beliefs, not so much because of perceived threats to job and wage security (although an indirect threat may be perceived by some) but because competition for other resources, such as schooling and housing, is increased.

Our effort is to state the theory in the broadest terms possible, thereby allowing its implications to be tested in as many diverse settings as is appropriate. The theory is stated explicitly in propositional form so that it can be proven incorrect—a practice all too frequently avoided by social theorists. We hope the theory will prove useful in its present or in altered form.

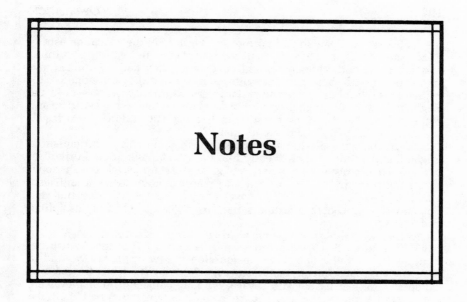

Notes

Chapter 1/The Nature of Oppression

1. Obviously, there are only degrees of "casteness." No social system totally inhibits mobility across ranks; some mobility always occurs. But in general, the less the mobility across ranks, the more confident we can be in labeling stratification processes in a society as a "caste system."

2. We are emphasizing that mobility occurs and is numerically frequent.

3. Of course, as Merton (1949) emphasized, the relationship between prejudice and discrimination is varied, since prejudice and discrimination can vary independently from each other.

4. Our analysis will be much different than some recent approaches to the topic. See, for the most conspicuous example of a varying approach, Lieberson (1980).

Chapter 2/The Culture of Black Oppression

1. While we drew upon several works in writing this historical overview of the culture of white racism, two monumental books were indispensable: Winthrop D. Jordan's *White Over Black* (1968), concerned with the roots of racism in England and America in the period from 1550 to 1812, and George M. Fredrickson's *The Black Image in the White Mind* (1971a), which analyzes racial beliefs in America from 1817 to 1914.

2. English racial attitudes at this time are generally regarded as far more virulent than Portuguese and Spanish attitudes, a fact that assumed crucial significance in the evolution of American and Latin American slavery. The difference appears to be due largely to two factors (Nash, 1970): (1) the geographical and cultural isolation of England and (2) the rise of Puritanism. Whereas the English had been relatively isolated from the rest of the world

191

for centuries, the Spanish and Portuguese, because of their location astride Europe and Africa, had been in continuous contact with a variety of cultures and races. As both conquerors and conquered, they had fraternized and intermarried with these peoples, with the result that they developed a tolerance for cultural diversity and racial intermixture that was absent in the English. By contrast, English insularity accentuated their ethnocentrism and made the racial and cultural differences that they encountered in Africa all the more striking and repugnant to them.

Strengthening these reactions were the effects of the rise of Puritanism in England at the time of English entry into the age of exploration. Puritanism can be seen as a response to a period of great social upheaval brought about by the transition from a feudal society to a more modern social order (Nash, 1970). In reaction to the crime, poverty, and other social problems that England experienced, the Puritans called for greater self-restraint, discipline, and control.

Given such an atmosphere, some historians (e.g., Jordan, 1968; Nash, 1970) have conjectured that Africans may have become a foil to the English, reminding them of attributes they subconsciously saw in themselves and in their society. Consequently, as Nash (1970:15) relates, "When Englishmen called the African bestial and savage, we may conjecture that they were unconsciously projecting onto black men qualities which they had identified and shrank from in themselves."

3. We should develop further two points about the evolution of slavery in the Americas. First, the fact that the English knew very little about the Spanish legal tradition of slavery possibly led them to misconstrue the nature of the enslavement that the Latins were practicing in the New World and may have caused the English to associate slavery with lifetime servitude for blacks. Under the Spanish legal tradition, slavery was viewed as an unfortunate accident that could happen to anyone, thereby preventing its identification exclusively with blacks. Moreover, slavery was essentially a contractual arrangement that extended certain rights to slaves and that regulated the powers of masters (see Tannenbaum, 1946:48-56). Secondly, although Indians were used as slaves by the Spanish and, for a very brief time, by the English, several factors worked against their permanent enslavement. Cultural experiences made Indians far less adaptable than Africans to farm labor. Indians often fell victim to European diseases against which Africans had acquired immunities. Tribal organization better enabled Indians to resist enslavement, and their familiarity with the terrain naturally made it easier for them to escape. Consequently, colonists came to value Indian trade and friendship more than their labor (cf. Marvin Harris, 1964:ch. 2).

4. North-south differences did not originate with the northern abolition of slavery. During the colonial era, southern colonies tended to enact harsher slave codes, to discriminate more against free blacks and to place greater restrictions on the private freeing of slaves. These policies were softened somewhat from the 1770s to the 1790s when the demand for slaves declined and slavery began to weigh more heavily on the American conscience. Several states in the Upper South followed the northern example at this time by passing laws facilitating the private liberation of slaves, an important development since such acts usually preceded emancipation acts in the North. However, as the number of free blacks in the Upper South swelled,

these states quickly took steps that reinforced their commitment to slavery. Tremendous restraints were placed upon free blacks, restrictions on the private freeing of slaves were retightened, and in the pivotal state of Virginia a law was passed in 1806 that demanded the emigration of all free blacks from the state within one year (Jordan, 1968).

The major factor in the reversal of the trend toward abolition in the Upper South was the proportion of blacks in the population (Jordan, 1968). In fact, in the North as well as the South, the pattern of resistance to abolition roughly corresponded to the percentage of blacks. The largest percentages in the North were in the last two states to pass emancipation laws, New York and New Jersey, while the first state to abolish slavery, Vermont, had very few blacks. Virginia and Maryland, where the proportion of blacks was large relative to the North but small to moderate compared to the rest of the South, were the only two southern states to seriously entertain thoughts of abolition. Apparently, the greater the number of blacks, the more threatening the prospect of abolition. Whites had long contended that free blacks were potential instigators of slave rebellion, and many expressed great alarm at an abortive slave revolt in Virginia in 1800 and at the triumph of black revolutionaries in Haiti during the same period. Whites also were undoubtedly apprehensive about giving up a system of control over blacks that they had held for generations. And, of course, the greater the proportion of blacks, the greater the vested economic interest in perpetuating slavery, an interest made even greater by the invention of the cotton gin in 1793. In short, the stakes were higher in the South where blacks were more numerous. Slave labor was assumed to be indispensable to the plantation economy, and emancipation was more of a threat to the established social order. In spite of their obvious sense of guilt over what was generally considered a "necessary evil," southerners simply could not bear the idea of relinquishing the institution of slavery.

5. Although proslavery apologists singlemindedly accepted the notion of black inferiority, not all of them justified slavery on this basis. A number of aristocratic planters, most notably George Fitzhugh, maintained that the South must be willing to defend slavery in general and not just for blacks. Attacking the fundamental assumptions of capitalism and democracy, Fitzhugh argued that the working class of advanced industrial societies like Great Britain would be better off under slavery. The patriarchal plantation was seen as the best model for society in general since it was ideally like a family, with benign masters tending the needs of their dependent children. The slaveholding intellectuals who espoused this view were such prolific defenders of slavery that their values have often been taken as representative of the South as a whole (see, e.g., Genovese, 1965). Some historians (Donald, 1971; Fredrickson, 1971a), however, question the influence of these arguments on the formation of public opinion in the era of Jacksonian democracy.

The nonslaveholding majority of antebellum white southerners, who acquired considerable political power after the extension of suffrage in the 1830s, saw slavery as a means of controlling the social and economic competition of blacks, and strongly opposed the reactionary class ideology of the large planters. The defense of slavery that most appealed to southern nonslaveholders (and also to northern sympathizers) defined the South as a *Herrenvolk* democracy, in which the egalitarian, natural-rights philosophy was a white racial prerogative based upon white racial superiority. Proponents of this view denounced the oppression of white laborers by an "aristocracy" that was not naturally superior to those it governed; and some went so far as to claim that true equality among whites could only exist alongside of black servitude (see Fredrickson, 1971a:ch. 2; McPherson, 1969).

6. The development of a sense of American nationalism in the eighteenth century, which culminated in the doctrine of "manifest destiny," revealed racist attitudes that went well beyond prejudice toward blacks. The Indian Removal Act of 1830 and subsequent genocidal policies toward Indians were designed to clear American lands for "American" (read white) civilization (see Borden, 1970). The debate that ensued after the Mexican War on whether to annex all of Mexico also focused on racial issues, with both sides taking racist positions. Proponents of "All Mexico" argued that "our free institutions" would in time "regenerate" the nonwhite races of Mexico, while opponents voiced fears of amalgamation with an "inferior" race unfit for self-government. The latter view—"that the American type of government is a white man's affair"—prevailed in 1848 and was a major deterrent to American expansionism for the next fifty years (Merk, 1963).

7. The failure to gain federal support as well as intense abolitionist opposition forced the colonization movement into the background after 1830. However, armed with the climatic theory of race, which held that blacks were suited for tropical climates and whites for temperate zones such as the United States, and supported by frustrated, pessimistic abolitionists, white nationalists revived interest in repatriation in the 1850s.

8. The series of constitutional amendments and civil rights acts passed after the war were motivated more by pragmatic, political ends than by moral persuasion. Arguments for equality morally appealed to the heritage of the natural-rights doctrine and to the performance of black troops to whom it was felt a debt was owed for their aid in preserving the Union. But more important were the political realities as defined by Northerners: Southern enfranchisement of blacks was thought to provide a means of preserving Republican supremacy and northern business interests, and it was felt that blacks would have no reason to move north if their freedom and welfare were protected by granting them basic civil rights. These motives lost some of their force in the 1870s, however, and when the presidential election of 1876 was disputed, federal troops were withdrawn from the South in return for the election of the Republican Hayes (see Woodward, 1968:89-107).

9. Following the Civil War, a new breed of southern paternalists emerged whose ideas were somewhat influential during the 1870s and 1880s. This group consisted of people such as Joel Chandler Harris, who spun several very popular nostalgic stories and novels about the Old South. It seems plausible that during this period of racial hatred and mistrust, these romantic tales of plantation slavery may have fed the ideas of black degeneracy to new generations of southern whites.

10. Northern "accommodation" to racial segregation in the South was consistent with the racialist rationale that emerged to justify American expansionism and with the reform philosophy of the so-called Progressive era. Expansionists defended the annexation of the Philippines, for example, by claiming that it was the "white man's burden" and the "missionary duty of

the civilized races" to uplift "people living in barbarism." Moreover, northern progressives advocated a philosophy of moderate reform that emphasized cooperation and noncoercive forms of "social control" (Fredrickson, 1971a: 305-19; Newby, 1965:13-16).

11. With respect to the concept of race, scientists now agree that: (1) All races belong to the same species—*Homo sapiens*. (2) Races are not discrete, stable units; that is, there are no "pure" races. (3) Races represent populations of people who share a common gene pool, or set of characteristics. (4) Thus, racial differences involve the relative frequency of genes, or traits, rather than absolute, mutually exclusive distinctions. (5) Race as a scientific concept has proven useless for the analysis of most human differences.

In the few instances where racial differences have been tied to different distributions of genes—such as in the analysis of blood types—the findings have underscored the adaptability and unity of mankind. For indeed, all races have demonstrated an equal potential for intelligence, an equal capacity to learn anything produced by any other race, and an equal capacity to adapt to the environment in which they live (see, for example, Osborne, 1971).

Chapter 3/Economic Oppression

1. Blacks were less likely to be counted than whites, since they were less likely to come into contact with those official agencies that would record population characteristics.

2. The Census Bureau has estimated that the slave population increased from about 1 million in 1790 to 4 million in 1860. Thus, this 1.5 million figure is probably conservative.

3. This fact runs counter to the modern, post-World War II situation where just the reverse is true (see figure 3.2).

4. Currently, about 22 percent of the total work force is unionized. This figure should be dramatically higher for blacks, since they are over 80 percent employed in blue-collar jobs, whereas less than 50 percent of white workers are in blue-collar jobs. (White-collar union membership only heightens the differences.)

Chapter 7/The Sociocultural Dynamics of Oppression

1. Examples of alternative theoretical explanations can be found in the following works: Allport (1954), Blauner (1972), Lieberson (1961, 1980), Noel (1968), Schermerhorn (1970), van den Berghe (1967), Williams (1947), William J. Wilson (1973), Averitt (1968), Bailey (1973), Baran and Sweezy (1966), Gordon (1972), Marvin Harris (1972), Reich (1981).

2. For applications of the split labor market theory to different empirical contexts, see Bonacich (1975, 1976).

3. While we recognize the existence of regional differences in antiblack attitudes throughout American history, we have chosen not to identify such differences in table 7.1 for several reasons. First, we believe that regional differences are largely a matter of degree and not of substance. Although antiblack prejudice has traditionally been more extreme in the South, the majority of Americans in all regions have ascribed to a similar set of beliefs about blacks, the basic tenet of which is black inferiority. Second, we thought

we should make as few a priori assumptions about sources of variation in beliefs as possible while constructing the table. Regional and other sources of belief variation are mentioned only insofar as they are commensurate with relevant categories, i.e., the structure of oppression, dominant beliefs, and "progressive" beliefs. Third, recent evidence (Middleton, 1976) from a national survey suggests that similar factors predispose people to racist beliefs in all regions. Finally, it is necessary to gloss over most intrasocietal variations in the interest of developing a macrolevel theory that pertains to society-wide processes of racial subordination and legitimation over a long span of history. Not only would it be too cumbersome to consider such variations at this stage in the development of the theory, but it seems desirable on heuristic grounds to sketch the theory before attending to potential anomalies suggested by regional and other sources of variation.

4. The theory discussed here is an expanded version of that presented in Turner and Singleton (1976).

5. While it may be argued that the early United States was not very democratic, most of the changes in racial oppression and beliefs considered here pertain to the period after which the United States became a formal political democracy.

6. The important operative here is "hold" or "adopt." It is not necessary that the threatened work force actually create legitimating racist beliefs, only that they accept such beliefs. Indeed, at various points in history, the dominant racist ideology has clearly been propagated by the "ruling" rather than the "working" class. It has been argued, for example, that the "positive good" theory of slavery was largely a creation of southern aristocrats (cf. Genovese, 1965). What was important for race relations in the antebellum South was that the racist elements in this ideology were almost universally accepted.

7. "Activism" stresses the appropriateness of individuals being able to master their environment; "achievement" stresses that individuals are to be free to strive for excellence and to excel; "individualism" maintains that people are to be free from external constraints; and "equality" underscores that people are to have equal chances to be active and achieve. We have modified, somewhat, Williams' terms, but the essence of his typology on these values is retained.

8. It can be argued, of course, that such core values legitimate capitalists' interests and the "oppressive arrangements" of a capitalist economy. To a considerable extent, such is no doubt the case, but nonetheless, these are the core values of capitalist systems. Action—whether for "good" or "bad"—is guided by them, and a theory of oppression must recognize their impact in the dynamics of oppressive arrangements.

Bibliography

Abernathy, Ralph D. "The Nonviolent Movement: The Past, the Present, and the Future." In *Black Life and Culture in the United States,* edited by R. L. Goldstein. New York: Thomas Crowell, 1971.

Allport, Gordon W. *The Nature of Prejudice.* Reading, Mass: Addison-Wesley, 1954.

Anderson, Bernard. "The Youth Unemployment Crisis." *Urban League Review,* 3 (Winter 1977): 16-21.

Antonovsky, Aaron. "The Social Meaning of Discrimination." *Phylon,* 21 (Spring 1960): 81-95.

Aptheker, Herbert. *The Negro in the Civil War.* New York: International Pub., 1938.

Averitt, Robert T. *The Dual Economy: The Dynamics of American Industry Structure.* New York: Norton, 1968.

Bailer, Lloyd H. "The Negro Automobile Worker." *Journal of Political Economy,* 51 (1943): 415-28.

_____. "The Automobile Unions and Negro Labor." *Political Science Quarterly,* 59 (1944): 548-77.

Bailey, Ron. "Economic Aspects of the Black Internal Colony." *Review of Black Political Economy,* 3 (1973): 43-72.

Banfield, Edward C. *The Unheavenly City.* Boston: Little, Brown, 1970.

Banfield, Edward C., and James Q. Wilson. *City Politics.* Cambridge, Mass.: Harvard University Press and M.I.T. Press, 1963.

Baran, Paul A., and Paul M. Sweezy. *Monopoly Capital.* New York: Monthly Review Press, 1966.

Barbour, Floyd B., ed. *The Black Power Revolt.* Boston: Porter Sargent, 1968.

Barnes, Harry E., and Negley K. Teeters. *New Horizons in Criminology.* 3d ed. Englewood Cliffs, N.J.: Prentice-Hall, 1959.

197

Berg, Ivar. *Education and Jobs: The Great Training Robbery.* Boston: Beacon Press, 1971.

Berry, Mary F. *Black Resistance/White Law.* New York: Appleton Press, 1971.

Berwanger, Eugene H. *The Frontier Against Slavery: Western Anti-Negro Prejudice and the Slavery Extension Controversy.* Urbana: University of Illinois Press, 1967.

Bestley, George R. *A History of the Freedmen's Bureau.* Philadelphia: University of Pennsylvania Press, 1955.

Blauner, Robert. *Racial Oppression in America.* New York: Harper and Row, 1972.

Boggs, James. *Racism and Class Struggle.* New York: Monthly Review Press, 1970.

Bonacich, Edna. "A Theory of Ethnic Antagonism: The Split Labor Market." *American Sociological Review,* 37 (1972): 547-59.

—————. "A Theory of Middleman Minorities." *American Sociological Review* 38 (1973): 583-94.

—————. "Advanced Capitalism and Black/White Relations in the United States: A Split Labor Market Interpretation." *American Sociological Review,* 41 (1976): 34-51.

—————. "Abolition, the Extension of Slavery, and the Position of Free Blacks: A Study of Split Labor Markets in the United States, 1830-1863." *American Journal of Sociology,* 81 (1978): 601-28.

Borden, Philip. "Found Cumbering the Soil: Manifest Destiny and the Indian in the Nineteenth Century." In *The Great Fear: Race in the Mind of America,* edited by B. Nash and R. Weiss. New York: Holt, Rinehart, and Winston, 1970.

Brawley, Benjamin. *A Short History of the American Negro.* 2d ed. New York: Macmillan, 1929.

Brimmer, Andrew. "The Negro in the National Economy." In *The American Negro Reference Book,* edited by P. David. Englewood Cliffs, N.J.: Prentice-Hall, 1966.

Brink, William, and Louis Harris. *Black and White.* New York: Simon and Schuster, 1966.

Brown, H. R. *Die Nigger Die!* New York: Dial Press, 1969.

Campbell, Angus. *White Attitudes Toward Black People.* Ann Arbor, Mich.: Institute for Social Research, 1971.

Campbell, Stanley W. *The Slave Catchers: Enforcement of the Fugitive Slave Law, 1850-1860.* Chapel Hill: University of North Carolina Press, 1970.

Cash, W. J. *The Mind of the South.* New York: Vintage Books, Knopf, 1941.

Chase, William M., and Peter Collier, eds. *Justice Denied: The Blackmen in White America.* New York: Harcourt, Brace, Jovanovich, 1970.

Cleaver, Eldridge. "Open Letter to Stokeley Carmichael." *Ramparts* 30 (Sept. 1969): 28-35.

Coleman, James S. et al. *Equality of Educational Opportunity.* Washington, D.C.: U.S. Government Printing Office, 1966.

Coombs, Orde. "Style Without the Substance of Power." *Black Enterprise,* 9 (Dec. 1978): 32-35.

Condran, John G. "Changes in White Attitudes Toward Blacks: 1963-1977." *Public Opinion Quarterly* 43, 4 (Winter 1979): 463-76.

Copeland, Lewis C. "The Negro as a Contrast Conception." In *Race Relations and the Race Problem*, edited by E.T. Thompson. Durham, N.C.: Duke University Press, 1939.

Copeland, Ronald S. "Community Origins of the Black Power Movement." In *Black Life and Culture in the United States*, edited by R.L. Goldstein. New York: Thomas Crowell, 1971.

Cox, Oliver C. "Leadership Among Negroes in the United States." In *Studies in Leadership*, edited by Alvin W. Gouldner. New York: Harper and Row, 1950.

Current Opinion, 3, No. 11:107. The Harris Survey, Aug. 30-Sept. 6, 1975.

Daniel, Pete. *The Shadow of Slavery: Peonage in the South 1901-1969*. London: Oxford University Press, 1973.

Davies, James C. *Processes of Rebellion: The History of Violence in America*. New York: Bantam, 1969.

Davis, James A. *General Social Surveys, 1972-1978: Cumulative Data*. New Haven: Roper Public Opinion Research Center, 1978.

Degler, Carl N. "Slavery and the Genesis of American Race Prejudice." *Comparative Studies in Society and History*, 2 (Oct. 1959): 49-66.

————. *Neither Black Nor White: Slavery and Race Relations in Brazil and the United States*. New York: Macmillan, 1971.

Delafosse, Maurice. *The Negroes of Africa: History and Culture*. Washington, D.C.: Associated Publishers, 1931.

Deutsch, Martin; Irwin Katz; and Arthur R. Jensen, eds. *Social Class, Race, and Psychological Development*. New York: Holt, Rinehart, and Winston, 1968.

Donald, David. *Lincoln Reconsidered: Essays on the Civil War Era*. New York: Knopf, 1956.

————. "The Proslavery Argument Reconsidered." *Journal of Southern History*, 37 (Feb. 1971): 3-18.

Douglass, Frederick. *The Life and Times of Frederick Douglass*. Cambridge, Mass.: Belknap Press, 1960.

Dreper, Theodore. *The Discovery of Black Nationalism*. New York: Viking Press, 1970.

Dubois, Shirley G. *His Day Is Marching On: A Memoir of W. E. B. Dubois*. New York: Lippincott, 1971.

Dubois, W. E. B. *Black Reconstruction in America*. New York: Harcourt, Brace, 1935.

Ellis, A. Caswell. *The Money Value of Education, Bulletin No. 22*. Dept. of the Interior, Bureau of Education, Washington, D.C.: U.S. Government Printing Office, 1971.

Erskine, Hazel. "The Polls: Negro Unemployment." *Public Opinion Quarterly*, 32 (1968a): 132-53.

————. "The Polls: Speed of Racial Integration." *Public Opinion Quarterly*, 32 (1968b): 513-24.

————. "The Polls: Recent Opinion on Racial Problems." *Public Opinion Quarterly*, 32 (1968c): 696-703.

Essien-Udom, E. U. *Black Nationalism*. Chicago: University of Chicago Press, 1962.

Farley, Reynolds; Howard Schuman; Suzanne Bianchi; Diane Colasanto; and Shirley Hatchett. " 'Chocolate City, Vanilla Suburbs': Will the Trend

Toward Racially Separate Communities Continue?" *Social Science Research* 7 (Dec. 1978):319-44.

Federal Bureau of Investigation. *Uniform Crime Reports, 1980.* Washington, D.C.: U.S. Government Printing Office, 1981.

Festinger, Leon. "A Theory of Social Comparison Processes." *Human Relations,* 7 (1954): 117-40.

————. *A Theory of Cognitive Dissonance.* Evanston, Ill.: Row, Peterson, 1957.

Fogel, Robert, and Stanley Engerman. *Time on the Cross.* Boston: Little, Brown, 1974.

Foley, Eugene P. "The Negro Businessman: In Search of a Tradition." In *The Negro American,* edited by T. Parsons and K. B. Clark. Boston: Beacon Press, 1966.

Foster, William Z. *The Negro People in American History.* New York: International Pub., 1959.

Franklin, John H. *Reconstruction After the Civil War.* Chicago: University of Chicago Press, 1961.

————. *From Slavery to Freedom: A History of Negro Americans.* 4th ed. New York: Knopf, 1974.

Frazier, E. Franklin. *Black Bourgeoisie.* New York: Free Press, 1957a.

————. *The Negro in the United States.* New York: Macmillan, 1957b.

————. *On Race Relations.* Chicago: University of Chicago Press, 1968.

Fredrickson, George M. *The Black Image in the White Mind: The Debate on Afro-American Character and Destiny, 1817-1914.* New York: Harper and Row, 1971a.

————. "Toward a Social Interpretation of the Development of American Racism." In *Key Issues in the Afro-American Experience,* Vol. 1, edited by I. Higgins, M. Kilson, and D. M. Fox. New York: Harcourt, Brace, Jovanovich, 1971b.

Gallup, George H. *The Gallup Poll: Public Opinion, 1935-1971.* Vol. 3. New York: Random House, 1972.

Gallup Opinion Index. Report No. 119, 1975.

Genovese, Eugene D. *The Political Economy of Slavery: Studies in the Economy and Society of the Slave South.* New York: Vintage Books, 1965.

Gibson, J. W., and W. H. Crogman. *Progress of a Race-or-the Remarkable Advancement of the American Negro,* 1902. Miami, Fla.: Mnemosyne Pub. Co., 1969.

Goldstein, Rhoda L., ed. *Black Life and Culture in the United States.* New York: Thomas Crowell, 1971.

Goode, Kenneth G. *From Africa to the United States and Then: A Concise Afro-American History.* 2d ed. Glenview, Ill.: Scott, Foresman, 1976.

Goodland, John I. "The School vs. Education." *Saturday Review,* 52 (Apr. 19, 1969): 59-61, 80-82.

Gordon, David M. *Theories of Poverty and Underemployment.* Lexington, Mass.: Heath, 1972.

Gossett, Thomas F. *Race: The History of an Idea in America.* Dallas, Tex.: Southern Methodist University Press, 1963.

Gottlieb, David. "Teaching and Students: The Views of Negro and White Teachers." *Sociology of Education,* 37 (Summer 1964): 345-53.

Government Research Corporation. "After the Votes Were Counted: A Campaign Potpourri." *National Journal,* 14, 45 (Nov. 1982): 1891.

Greeley, Andrew M., and Paul B. Sheatsley. "Attitudes Toward Racial Integration." *Scientific American,* 225 (Dec. 1971): 13-19.
Greene, Lorenzo J., and Carter G. Woodson. *The Negro Wage Earner.* Washington, D.C.: Association for the Study of Negro Life and History, Inc., 1930.
Haller, John S., Jr. *Outcasts from Evolution: Scientific Attitudes of Racial Inferiority, 1859-1900.* Urbana: University of Illinois Press, 1971.
Hamilton, C. Horace. "The Negro Leaves the South." *Demography,* 1,1 (1964): 273-95.
Handlin, Oscar, and Mary F. Handlin. "Origins of the Southern Labor System." *William and Mary Quarterly,* 3d Series, 7 (Apr. 1950): 199-222.
Harris, A. L. *The Black Worker: The Negro and the Labor Movement.* New York: Columbia University Press, 1931.
Harris, Donald J. "The Black Ghetto as Colony: A Theoretical Critique and Alternative Formulation." *Review of Black Political Economy,* 2 (1972): 3-33.
Harris, Marvin. *Patterns of Race in the Americas.* New York: Walker and Co., 1964.
Helm, Mary. *From Darkness to Light: The Story of Negro Progress,* 1909. New York: Negro University Press, 1969.
Henry, Charles P. "Big Philanthropy and the Funding of Black Organizations." *Review of Black Political Economy,* 19 (Winter 1979): 174-90.
Hill, Robert B. "The Economic Status of Black Families." In *The State of Black America: 1979.* New York: National Urban League, 1979.
Hindelang, Michael J. et al. *Sourcebook of Criminal Justice Statistics,* NCJIS Report No. SD-SB-4. Washington, D.C.: U.S. Government Printing Office, 1977.
Hinds, Lennox S. "The Relevance of the Past to the Present: A Political Interpretation." In *Black Life and Culture in the United States,* edited by R. L. Goldstein. New York: Thomas Y. Crowell, 1971.
Holsendolph, Ernest. "Blacks Can't Bank on Conventional Loans." *Black Enterprise,* 9 (Jan. 1979): 19-21.
Hughes, Langston. *Fight for Freedom: The Story of the N.A.A.C.P.* New York: W. W. Norton, 1962.
Hyman, Herbert H., and Paul B. Sheatsley. "Attitudes Toward Desegregation." *Scientific American,* 211 (Dec. 1964): 2-9.
Jacobsen, Julius. *The Negro and the American Labor Movement.* New York: Doubleday, 1968.
Jencks, Christopher, et al. *Inequality: A Reassessment of the Effect of Family and Schooling in America.* New York: Basic Books, 1972.
Jenkins, William S. *Pro-Slavery Thought in the Old South.* Chapel Hill: University of North Carolina Press, 1935.
Johnson, Edward A. *A School History of the Negro Race in America: 1916-1890, 1911.* New York: AMS Press, 1969.
Johnson, Guion. "The Ideology of White Supremacy, 1875-1910." In *Essays in Southern History,* edited by F. M. Green. Chapel Hill: University of North Carolina Press, 1949.
Johnson, Guy. "The Negro and Crime." *The Annals, American Academy of Political and Social Science,* 217 (Sept. 1941): 93-104.
Joint Center for Political Studies. *National Roster of Black Elected Officials,* vol. 10 (1980). Washington, D.C.: Joint Center for Political Studies, 1981.

Jones, James M. *Prejudice and Racism.* Reading, Mass.: Addison-Wesley, 1972.

Jones, Robert H. *Disrupted Decades: The Civil War and Reconstruction Years.* New York: Scribner's, 1973.

Jordan, Winthrop D. "Modern Tensions and the Origins of American Slavery." *Journal of Southern History,* 28 (Feb. 1962): 18-30.

————. *White Over Black: American Attitudes Toward the Negro, 1550-1812.* Chapel Hill: University of North Carolina Press, 1968.

Killian, Lewis M. *The Impossible Revolution, Phase 2: Black Power and the American Dream.* New York: Random House, 1975.

Kincaid, Larry. "Two Steps Forward, One Step Back: Racial Attitudes During the Civil War and Reconstruction." In *The Great Fear: Race in the Mind of America,* edited by G. B. Nash and R. Weiss. New York: Holt, Rinehart, and Winston, 1970.

Kinder, Donald R., and David O. Sears. "Prejudice and Politics: Symbolic Racism versus Racial Threats to 'The Good Life.' " *Journal of Personality and Social Psychology,* 40 (1981): 414-31.

Kirkman, Joseph M. "A White Teacher in a Negro School." *Journal of Negro Education,* 35 (Spring 1966): 178-79.

Knowles, Louis L., and Kenneth Prewitt. *Institutional Racism in America.* Englewood Cliffs, N.J.: Prentice-Hall, 1969.

Kozol, Jonathan. *Death at an Early Age.* New York: Houghton-Mifflin, 1967.

Lee, Ulysses. *U.S. Army in World War II: The Deployment of Negro Troops.* Washington, D.C.: U.S. Army, Office of the Chief of Military History, 1966.

Levine, Robert A. "The Silent Majority: Neither Simple Nor Simple-Minded." *Public Opinion Quarterly,* 35 (1971-72): 571-77.

Lieberson, Stanley. "A Societal Theory of Race and Ethnic Relations." *American Sociological Review,* 26 (1961): 902-10.

————. *A Piece of the Pie: Black and White Immigrants Since 1880.* Berkeley: University of California Press, 1980.

Lincoln, C. Eric. *The Black Muslims in America.* Boston: Beacon Press, 1961.

Lipset, Seymour M., and William Schneider. "The Bakke Case: How Would It Be Decided at the Bar of Public Opinion." *Public Opinion,* 1 (Mar./Apr. 1978):38-44.

Litwack, Leon F. *North of Slavery: The Negro in the Free States, 1790-1860.* Chicago: University of Chicago Press, 1961.

Marcus, Lloyd. *The Treatment of Minorities in Secondary School Textbooks.* New York: Anti-Defamation League, 1961.

Marine, Gene. *The Black Panthers.* New York: New American Library, 1969.

Marshall, Ray. *The Negro and Organized Labor.* New York: Wiley, 1965.

McKitrick, Eric L. *Slavery Defended: The Views of the Old South.* Englewood Cliffs, N.J.: Prentice-Hall, 1963.

McPherson, James. M. *The Struggle for Equality: Abolitionists and the Negro in the Civil War and Reconstruction.* Princeton, N.J.: Princeton University Press, 1964.

————. "Slavery and Race." *Perspectives in American History,* 3 (1969):460-73.

Mecklin, John M. *The Ku Klux Klan: A Study of the American Mind.* New York: Harcourt, Brace, 1924.

Meier, August. *Negro Thought in America, 1880-1915.* Ann Arbor: University of Michigan Press, 1963.

Merk, Fredrick. *Manifest Destiny and Mission in American History: A Reinterpretation.* New York: Knopf, 1963.

Merton, Robert K. "Discrimination and The American Creed." In *Discrimination and National Welfare,* edited by R. M. McIver. New York: Harper and Row, 1949.

Middleton, Russell. "Regional Differences in Prejudice." *American Sociological Review,* 41(1976): 94-117.

Miller, Loren. "Race, Poverty and the Law." In *Aspects of Poverty,* edited by E. B. Seligman. New York: Thomas Crowell, 1968.

Morris, Milton D. *The Politics of Black America.* New York: Harper and Row, 1975.

Muhammed, Elijah. *Message to the Blackmen in America.* Chicago: Muhammed Mosque of Islam, No. 2, 1965.

Mullen, Robert. *Blacks in American Wars.* New York: Monad Press, 1973.

Myrdal, Gunner. *An American Dilemma,* vol. 2. New York: Harper and Row, 1944.

Nash, Gary B. "Red, White, and Black: The Origins of Racism in Colonial America." In *The Great Fear: Race in the Mind of America,* edited by G. B. Nash and R. Weiss. New York: Holt, Rinehart and Winston, 1970.

National Bar Association Judicial Council Report. Presented at the mid-year conference, St. Croix, Virgin Islands, 1982.

National Urban League. "Some Facts about Black Youth." *Urban League Review,* 3 (Winter 1977): 37-38.

Newby, Idus A. *Jim Crow's Defense: Anti-Negro Thought in America, 1900-1930.* Baton Rouge: Louisiana State University Press, 1965.

Newsweek. "The Troubled American: A Special Report on the White Majority." *Newsweek,* July 12, 1969, pp. 29-73.

Noel, Donald L. "A Theory of the Origin of Ethnic Stratification." *Social Problems,* 16 (1968): 157-72.

Northrup, Herbert R. *Organized Labor and The Negro.* New York: Harper, 1944.

Osborne, Richard H., ed. *The Biological and Social Meaning of Race.* San Francisco: W. H. Freeman, 1971.

Parris, Guichard, and Lester Brooks. *Blacks in the City: A History of the National Urban League.* Boston: Little, Brown, 1971.

Parsons, Talcott. "The School Class as a Social System: Some of Its Functions in American Society." *Harvard Educational Review,* 24 (Fall 1959): 297-318.

Perlo, Victor. *The Economics of Racism.* New York: International Pub., 1975.

Pettigrew, Thomas F. *A Profile of the Negro American.* Princeton: Van Nostrand, 1964.

————. *Racial Isolation in the Public Schools,* vol. 1. Washington, D.C.: U.S. Government Printing Office, 1967.

————. "Racially Separate or Together?" *Journal of Social Issues,* 25 (1969a): 43-69.

————. "The Negro and Education: Problems and Proposals." In *Race and the Social Sciences,* edited by I. Katz and P. Gurin. New York: Basic Books, 1969b.

Pinkney, Alphonso. *Black Americans*. Englewood Cliffs, N.J.: Prentice-Hall, 1969.

_____. "Contemporary Black Nationalism." In *Black Life and Culture in the United States*, edited by R. L. Goldstein. New York: Thomas Crowell, 1971.

Piovia, Esther. "Black Youth Unemployment: A Continuing Crisis." *Urban League Review*, 3 (Winter 1977): 40-45.

Polski, Harry A., and Ernest Kaiser, eds. *The Negro Almanac*. 2d ed. New York: Bellwhether, 1971.

Quarles, Benjamin. *The Negro in the Civil War*. Boston: Little, Brown, 1953.

_____. *Lincoln and the Negro*. New York: Oxford University Press, 1962.

Quinney, Richard. *Criminology*. 2d ed. Boston: Little, Brown, 1979.

Raab, Earl, and Seymour M. Lipset. "The Prejudiced Society." In *American Race Relations Today*, edited by E. Raab. Garden City, N.Y.: Doubleday, 1962.

Raper, A. *The Tragedy of Lynching*. Chapel Hill: University of North Carolina Press, 1933.

Reich, Michael. *Racial Inequality: A Political-Economic Analysis*. Princeton, N.J.: Princeton University Press, 1981.

Reid, Sue Titus. *Crime and Criminology*. 2d ed. New York: Holt, Rinehart and Winston, 1979.

Rist, Ray C. "Student Social Class and Teacher Expectations: The Self-fulfilling Prophecy In Ghetto Education." *Harvard Educational Review*, 40 (Aug. 1970): 411-51.

Robinson, Theodore P., and Thomas R. Dye. "Reformism and Black Representation on City Councils." *Social Science Quarterly*, 59 (June 1978): 133-41.

Rose, Peter I. *The Subject Is Race*. New York: Oxford University Press, 1968.

Rosenthal, Robert, and Lenore Jacobson. *Pygmalion in the Classroom: Teacher Expectations and Pupil Intellectual Development*. New York: Holt, Rinehart, and Winston, 1968a.

_____. "Teacher Expectations For the Disadvantaged." *Scientific American*, 218 (Apr. 1968b): 3-7.

Rowan, Carl T. *Just Between Us Blacks*. New York: Random House, 1974.

Saunders, Doris E., and *Ebony* staff, eds. *The Ebony Handbook*, Chicago: Johnson Pub., 1974.

Schaffler, Albert, et al. *Understanding Social Problems*. Columbus, Ohio: Charles E. Merrill, 1970.

Scheer, Robert, ed. *Eldridge Cleaver: Post-Prison Speeches and Writings*. New Haven, Conn.: Yale University Press, 1969.

Schermerhorn, Robert A. *Comparative Ethnic Relations: A Framework for Theory and Research*. New York: Random House, 1970.

Schuman, Howard. "Sociological Racism." *Trans-Action*, 7 (Jan. 1969): 44-48.

Schwartz, Mildred A. *Trends in White Attitudes toward Negroes*. Chicago: National Opinion Research Center, 1967.

Seale, Bobby. *Seize the Time: The Story of the Black Panther Party and Huey P. Newton*. New York: Random House, 1970.

Sears, David O.; Carl P. Hensler; and Leslie K. Speer. "Whites' Opposition to 'Busing': Self-Interest or Symbolic Politics?" *American Political Science Review*, 73 (June 1979): 369-84.

Sheatsley, Paul B. "White Attitudes toward the Negro." *Daedalus*, 95 (1966): 217-38.

Simms, Margaret C. "The Economy: 1978." In *The State of Black America: 1979.* New York: National Urban League, 1979.

Simon, Rita James. *Public Opinion in America: 1936-1970.* Chicago: Rand-McNally, 1974.

Simpson, George E., and J. Milton Yinger. *Racial and Cultural Minorities: An Analysis of Prejudice and Discrimination.* 4th ed. New York: Harper and Row, 1972.

Singleton, Royce, Jr., and Jonathan H. Turner. "Racism: White Oppression of Blacks in America." In *Understanding Social Problems*, edited by D. H. Zimmerman, D. L. Wieder, and S. Zimmerman. New York: Praeger, 1976.

Sloan, Irving. *The Negro in Modern History Textbooks.* 2d ed. Washington, D.C.: American Federation of Teachers, AFL-CIO, 1967.

Spero, Sterling D., and Abran L. Harris. *The Black Worker.* Port Washington, N.Y.: Kennikat Press, 1931.

Stampp, Kenneth M. *The Peculiar Institution: Slavery in the Ante-Bellum South.* New York: Vintage Books, 1956.

Stanton, William. *The Leopard's Spots: Scientific Attitudes Toward Race in America 1815-59.* Chicago: University of Chicago Press, 1960.

Starobin, Robert S. *Industrial Slavery in the Old South.* London: Oxford University Press, 1970.

Stent, Madelon D. "Education for Black Americans On the 25th Anniversary of the Brown Decision." In *The State of Black America: 1979.* New York: National Urban League, 1979.

Taeuber, Karl E., and Alma F. Taeuber. *Negroes in Cities.* Chicago: Aldine, 1965.

Takaki, Ronald. "The Black Child-Savage in Ante-Bellum America." In *The Great Fear: Race in the Mind of America*, edited by G. B. Nash and R. Weiss. New York: Holt, Rinehart and Winston, 1970.

Tannenbaum, Frank. *Slave and Citizen: The Negro in the Americas.* New York: Knopf, 1946.

Taylor, D. Garth; Paul B. Sheatsley; and Andrew M. Greeley. "Attitudes Toward Racial Integration." *Scientific American*, 238 (June 1978):42-49.

Thirty Years of Lynching, 1889-1918. New York: NAACP, 1919.

Thomas, Tony. *Black Liberation and Socialism.* New York: Pathfinder Press, 1974.

Thomas, William I. "The Psychology of Race-Prejudice." *American Journal of Sociology*, 9 (Mar. 1904): 593-611.

Turner, Jonathan H. *Patterns of Social Organization.* New York: McGraw-Hill, 1972.

————. *Social Problems in America.* New York: Harper and Row, 1976a.

————. *American Society: Problems of Structure.* New York: Harper and Row, 1976b.

————. *Sociology: Studying The Human System.* Santa Monica, Calif.: Goodyear, 1978.

————. *Societal Stratification: A Theoretical Analysis.* New York: Columbia University Press, 1984.

Turner, Jonathan H., and Edna Bonacich. "Toward a Composite Theory of

Middleman Minorities." *Ethnicity* (Fall 1980): 144-58.

Turner, Jonathan H., and Royce Singleton, Jr. "A Theory of Ethnic Oppression: Toward a Re-integration of Cultural and Structural Concepts in Ethnic Relations Theory." *Social Forces*, 56 (Mar. 1976): 1001-8.

Turner, Jonathan H., and Charles E. Starnes, *Inequality: Privilege and Poverty in America*. Santa Monica, Calif.: Goodyear, 1976.

Turner, Ralph. "Sponsored and Contest Mobility in the School System." *American Sociological Review*, 25 (Dec. 1960): 855-67.

U.S. Commission on Civil Disorders. *Report of the National Advisory Commission on Civil Disorders*. New York: Bantam, 1968.

U.S. Commission on Civil Rights. *Civil Rights U.S.A.-Public Schools, Southern States*. Washington, D.C.: U.S. Government Printing Office, 1967.

U.S. Department of Commerce, Bureau of the Census. *Negro Population in the United States: 1790-1905*. Washington, D.C.: U.S. Government Printing Office, 1918.

_____. *Voting and Registration in the Election of November, 1980*, Series P. 20, No. 359, Current Population Reports. Washington, D.C.: U.S. Government Printing Office, 1981.

_____. *The Social and Economic Status of the Black Population in the U.S.: An Historical View, 1790-1978*, Series P-23, No. 80, Current Population Reports. Washington, D.C.: U.S. Government Printing Office, 1979a.

_____. *Ancestry and Language in the United States*, Series P-23, No. 116, Current Population Reports. Washington, D.C.: U.S. Government Printing Office, 1979b.

_____. *Population Profile of the United States: 1981*, Series P-20, No. 374, Current Population Reports. Washington, D.C.: U.S. Government Printing Office, 1982.

U.S. Department of Education. *Digest of Education Statistics*. Washington, D.C.: U.S. Government Printing Office, 1979.

_____. *The American High School: A Statistical Overview*. Washington, D.C.: U.S. Government Printing Office, 1980.

_____. *Digest of Education Statistics*. Washington, D.C.: U.S. Government Printing Office, 1982.

U.S. Department of Justice, Federal Bureau of Prisons. *Statistical Report*. Washington, D.C.: U.S. Government Printing Office, 1979.

U.S. Department of Labor, Bureau of Labor Statistics. *Monthly Labor Review*, Vol. 105, No. 12 (Dec. 1982).

U.S. Supreme Court. *Brown v. Board of Education of Topeka* (1954).

_____. *Green v. County School Board of New Kent County* (1968).

_____. *Swann v. Board of Education of Charlotte-Mecklenburg County* (1971).

U.S. War Department and John Davis, eds. *The American Negro Reference Book*. Englewood Cliffs, N.J.: Prentice-Hall, 1966.

van der Berghe, Pierre L. *Race and Racism: A Comparative Perspective*. New York: Wiley, 1967.

Vander Zanden, James. *American Minority Relations*. New York: Ronald Press, 1972.

Vincent, Theodore G. *Black Power and the Garvey Movement*. Berkeley, Calif.: Ramparts Press, 1971.

Walter, Raymond. *Negroes and the Great Depression.* Westport, Conn.: Greenwood Pub. Co., 1970.

Washington, Booker T. *The Negro in the South: His Economic Progress in Relation to His Morale and Political Development.* London: T. Fisher Unwin, 1909.

————. *Up from Slavery.* New York: Doubleday, 1933.

Weinberg, Meyer. *Race and Place: A Legal History of the Neighborhood School.* Washington, D.C.: U.S. Government Printing Office, 1968.

————. *A Chance to Learn: The History of Race and Education in the United States.* New York: Cambridge University Press, 1977.

Welch, Susan, and Albert K. Karnig. "Representation of Blacks on Big City School Boards." *Social Science Quarterly,* 59 (June 1978): 162-72.

Wesley, Charles. *Negro Labor in the United States.* New York: Vanguard Press, 1927.

Westie, Frank R. "Race and Ethnic Relations." In *Handbook of Modern Sociology,* edited by R. E. L. Faris. Chicago: Rand-McNally, 1964.

Weston, Rubin F. *Racism in U.S. Imperialism: The Influence of Racial Assumptions in American Foreign Policy, 1893-1946.* Columbia: University of South Carolina Press, 1972.

Williams, Dennis A.; Jerry Buckley; and Mary Lord. "A New Racial Poll." *Newsweek.* Feb. 26, 1979, pp. 48, 53.

Williams, Eddie N. "Black Political Participation in 1978." In *The State of Black America: 1979.* New York: National Urban League, 1979.

Williams, Robin M. *The Reduction of Intergroup Tensions: A Survey of Research on Problems of Ethnic, Racial, and Religious Group Relations.* New York: Russell Sage Foundation, 1947.

————. *Strangers Next Door: Ethnic Relations in American Communities.* Englewood Cliffs, N.J.: Prentice-Hall, 1964.

————. *American Society: A Sociological Interpretation.* 2d ed. New York: Knopf, 1970.

Wilson, Alan B. *The Effect of Residential Segregation Upon Educational Achievement and Aspirations.* Doctoral dissertation, University of California, Berkeley, 1960.

Wilson, Theodore B. *The Black Codes of the South.* University, Ala.: University of Alabama Press, 1965.

Wilson, William J. *Power, Racism, and Privilege: Race Relations: Theoretical and Sociohistorical Perspectives.* New York: Macmillan, 1973.

Woodson, G. Carter. *The African Background Outline.* Washington, D.C.: Associated Pub., 1936.

Woodward, C. Vann. *The Strange Career of Jim Crow.* 2d ed. New York: Oxford University Press, 1966.

————. *The Burden of Southern History.* Rev. ed. Baton Rouge: Louisiana State University Press, 1968.

Zilversmit, Arthur. *The First Emancipation: The Abolition of Slavery in the North.* Chicago: University of Chicago Press, 1967.

Index

Name index

Abernathy, Ralph D., 80, 98, 99
Allport, Gordon W., 195n
Anderson, Bernard, 63
Averitt, Robert T., 195n

Bailey, Ron, 195n
Banfield, Edward C., 126
Baran, Paul A., 195n
Benezet, Anthony, 17
Berg, Ivar, 137
Berwanger, Eugene H., 22
Best, George, 12
Bianchi, Suzanne, 38
Blauner, Robert, 169, 176, 195n
Boas, Franz, 32, 183
Bonacich, Edna, 3, 6, 7, 55, 168, 169,
    179, 180, 195n
Borden, Philip, 194n
Brawley, Benjamin, 117, 119
Brimmer, Andrew, 59
Brink, William, 176
Brooke, Edward, 101
Buckley, Jerry, 35, 36

Campbell, Angus, 176
Cash, W. J., 117
Cleaver, Eldridge, 73, 102
Colasanto, Diane, 38
Coleman, James S., 132–33, 138
Condran, John G., 37, 38
Coolidge, Calvin, 72

Cornish, Samuel E., 79–80
Cox, Oliver C., 70
Crogman, W. H., 121–22

Davis, James A., 39, 40
Degler, Carl N., 14, 71
Deutsch, Martin, 176
Donald, David, 183, 193n
Douglas, Frederick, 70, 80, 81, 85, 88,
    95, 161
Douglas, Stephen, 82
Dubois, W. E. B., 70, 85, 91, 99–100,
    149, 159

Ellis, A. Caswell, 137
Engerman, Stanley, 44
Erskine, Hazel, 176

Farley, Reynolds, 38
Fitzhugh, George, 193n
Fogel, Robert, 44
Foley, Eugene P., 59
Foster, William Z., 72, 74, 79, 92, 93,
    96, 159, 160, 161
Franklin, John H., 72, 74, 83, 92, 146,
    176
Frazier, E. Franklin, 91, 125, 149, 176
Frederickson, George M., 14, 19, 20, 21,
    24, 26, 27, 28, 33, 176, 191n, 193n,
    194n, 195n

Subject index